Unemployment

Other Books of Related Interest:

Opposing Viewpoints Series

The Achievement Gap

The Banking Crisis

Debt

At Issue Series

Are America's Wealthy Too Powerful?

Do Tax Breaks Benefit the Economy?

Current Controversies Series

Jobs in America

The U.S. Economy

The World Economy

"Congress shall make no law . . . abridging the freedom of speech, or of the press."

First Amendment to the U.S. Constitution

The basic foundation of our democracy is the First Amendment guarantee of freedom of expression. The *Opposing Viewpoints* Series is dedicated to the concept of this basic freedom and the idea that it is more important to practice it than to enshrine it.

Unemployment

David Haugen and Susan Musser, Book Editors

GREENHAVEN PRESS
A part of Gale, Cengage Learning

Detroit • New York • San Francisco • New Haven, Conn • Waterville, Maine • London

GALE
CENGAGE Learning™

Christine Nasso, *Publisher*
Elizabeth Des Chenes, *Managing Editor*

For more information, contact:
Greenhaven Press
27500 Drake Rd.
Farmington Hills, MI 48331-3535
Or you can visit our Internet site at gale.cengage.com

Articles in Greenhaven Press anthologies are often edited for length to meet page requirements. In addition, original titles of these works are changed to clearly present the main thesis and to explicitly indicate the author's opinion. Every effort is made to ensure that Greenhaven Press accurately reflects the original intent of the authors. Every effort has been made to trace the owners of copyrighted material.

LIBRARY OF CONGRESS CATALOGING-IN-PUBLICATION DATA

Unemployment / David Haugen and Susan Musser, book editors.
p. cm. -- (Opposing viewpoints)
Includes bibliographical references and index.
ISBN 978-0-7377-5247-2 (hbk.) -- ISBN 978-0-7377-5248-9 (pbk.)
1. Unemployment--United States--Juvenile literature. 2. Manpower policy--United States--Juvenile literature. I. Haugen, David M., 1969- II. Musser, Susan.
HD5724.U593 2011
331.13'7973--dc22

2010043794

Printed in the United States of America
1 2 3 4 5 6 7 15 14 13 12 11

Contents

Why Consider Opposing Viewpoints?

> *"The only way in which a human being can make some approach to knowing the whole of a subject is by hearing what can be said about it by persons of every variety of opinion and studying all modes in which it can be looked at by every character of mind. No wise man ever acquired his wisdom in any mode but this."*
>
> *John Stuart Mill*

In our media-intensive culture it is not difficult to find differing opinions. Thousands of newspapers and magazines and dozens of radio and television talk shows resound with differing points of view. The difficulty lies in deciding which opinion to agree with and which "experts" seem the most credible. The more inundated we become with differing opinions and claims, the more essential it is to hone critical reading and thinking skills to evaluate these ideas. Opposing Viewpoints books address this problem directly by presenting stimulating debates that can be used to enhance and teach these skills. The varied opinions contained in each book examine many different aspects of a single issue. While examining these conveniently edited opposing views, readers can develop critical thinking skills such as the ability to compare and contrast authors' credibility, facts, argumentation styles, use of persuasive techniques, and other stylistic tools. In short, the Opposing Viewpoints Series is an ideal way to attain the higher-level thinking and reading skills so essential in a culture of diverse and contradictory opinions.

In addition to providing a tool for critical thinking, *Opposing Viewpoints* books challenge readers to question their own strongly held opinions and assumptions. Most people form their opinions on the basis of upbringing, peer pressure, and personal, cultural, or professional bias. By reading carefully balanced opposing views, readers must directly confront new ideas as well as the opinions of those with whom they disagree. This is not to simplistically argue that everyone who reads opposing views will—or should—change his or her opinion. Instead, the series enhances readers' understanding of their own views by encouraging confrontation with opposing ideas. Careful examination of others' views can lead to the readers' understanding of the logical inconsistencies in their own opinions, perspective on why they hold an opinion, and the consideration of the possibility that their opinion requires further evaluation.

Evaluating Other Opinions

To ensure that this type of examination occurs, *Opposing Viewpoints* books present all types of opinions. Prominent spokespeople on different sides of each issue as well as well-known professionals from many disciplines challenge the reader. An additional goal of the series is to provide a forum for other, less known, or even unpopular viewpoints. The opinion of an ordinary person who has had to make the decision to cut off life support from a terminally ill relative, for example, may be just as valuable and provide just as much insight as a medical ethicist's professional opinion. The editors have two additional purposes in including these less known views. One, the editors encourage readers to respect others' opinions—even when not enhanced by professional credibility. It is only by reading or listening to and objectively evaluating others' ideas that one can determine whether they are worthy of consideration. Two, the inclusion of such viewpoints encourages the important critical thinking skill of objectively evaluating an author's credentials and bias. This evaluation will illuminate an author's reasons for taking a particular stance on an issue and will aid in readers' evaluation of the author's ideas.

It is our hope that these books will give readers a deeper understanding of the issues debated and an appreciation of the complexity of even seemingly simple issues when good and honest people disagree. This awareness is particularly important in a democratic society such as ours in which people enter into public debate to determine the common good. Those with whom one disagrees should not be regarded as enemies but rather as people whose views deserve careful examination and may shed light on one's own.

Thomas Jefferson once said that "difference of opinion leads to inquiry, and inquiry to truth." Jefferson, a broadly educated man, argued that "if a nation expects to be ignorant and free . . . it expects what never was and never will be." As individuals and as a nation, it is imperative that we consider the opinions of others and examine them with skill and discernment. The *Opposing Viewpoints* Series is intended to help readers achieve this goal.

David L. Bender and Bruno Leone,
Founders

Introduction

> *"The first quarter of this year, we were losing jobs at an average of 700,000 jobs per month, month after month. In the quarter that ended this week, the loss was 250,000 jobs per month, two-thirds less. . . . We don't think that 'less bad' is good. 'Less bad' is not our measure of success. One job lost is one job too many, and it's still too much pain."*
>
> *—Vice President Joe Biden, White House speech on unemployment, October 2, 2009*

> *"Private payroll employment has risen an average of 140,000 per month for the past three months, and expectations of both businesses and households about hiring prospects have improved since the beginning of the year. In all likelihood, however, a significant amount of time will be required to restore the nearly 8-1/2 million jobs that were lost over 2008 and 2009."*
>
> *—Federal Reserve Chairman Ben S. Bernanke, testimony before the U.S. House of Representatives Committee on the Budget, June 9, 2010*

Between 2006 and 2008, years of easy credit and subprime mortgages caught up with banking institutions when the U.S. housing market collapsed. The failure of banks to recoup their bad investments triggered a shockwave in the economy that resulted in the tightening of credit, the depreciation of stock, and the bankruptcy of many businesses. The nation fell into a financial recession that took its toll on the American workforce as well. With massive layoffs and hiring freezes, businesses thinned out their staffs to weather the crisis. By October 2009, the national unemployment rate in the United States was 10.1 percent, the highest it had been in 26 years and nearly twice the rate in the years preceding the recession.

The White House reacted to the financial crisis by buying some bad assets (home loans, etc.) from banks to entice them to begin lending money again to businesses in hopes that the new capital would lead to the expansion of employment opportunities. President Barack Obama also helped orchestrate a monetary stimulus program to cut interest rates, inaugurate tax cuts, and lend money directly to businesses to speed recovery. The $787 billion American Recovery and Reinvestment Act eventually passed Congress in February 2009, but its effects are still the subject of popular and partisan debate. Some liberals argue that the stimulus package should have been larger; conservatives tend to believe the increase in the national debt and government intervention in the marketplace are obvious outcomes that should have persuaded lawmakers to steer clear of the bill. Jackie Calmes and Michael Cooper of the *New York Times* reported on November 20, 2009, that "a broad range of economists said the White House and Congress were right to structure the package as a mix of tax cuts and spending, rather than just tax cuts as Republicans prefer or just spending as many Democrats do." Regardless, the stimulus may be propping up some industries, but the growth of these businesses has not put a significant dent in the unemployment rate, prompting analysts and pundits to call the slow march out of the recession a "jobless recovery." Though economists might be pleased to interpret any growth in the country's gross domestic product as a good sign, CBS *MoneyWatch* reporter John Keefe noted in a January 14, 2010, posting, "The way I see it, if jobs aren't being created, then the economy is probably not on the mend."

The national unemployment levels have fluctuated slightly since October 2009, with each minor gain encouraging some observers to forecast an end to the crisis. By the end of that year, unemployment remained at 10 percent—a gloomy figure but not as devastating as the rate endured during the Great Depression of the 1930s, which at its worst reached nearly 25 percent and, even just before its end, hovered at around 15 percent. However, the U.S. Bureau of Labor Statistics (BLS) noted that the 2009 unemployment rate did not reveal all of the ominous aspects of the current recession. According to the BLS, 4 in 10 unemployed persons (about 6.1 million workers) had been jobless for 27 weeks or more, a record high since such statistics were first compiled in 1948. In addition, the bureau reported that "only 17 percent of all the unemployed in one month found jobs by the next month, compared with about 28 percent of the unemployed in 2007." The national average also does not indicate the bleakness of some regional unemployment figures. Even in June 2010, when the country's unemployment rate dropped to 9.7 percent, 134 metropolitan areas still suffered double-digit unemployment figures, including centers of declining auto manufacturing such as Flint, Michigan (14.7 percent), and Detroit (13.7 percent).

Even in these times of high unemployment, job creation is taking place. In the first five months of 2010, the U.S. economy added 500,000 jobs, prompting some economists to trumpet a reversal of fortunes. "The economy has been in a recovery since the middle of last year," Stuart G. Hoffman, chief economist for the PNC Financial Services Group, told the *Washington Post* for a May 8, 2010, article. "For that recovery to turn into an expansion and to be self-sustaining, there has to be job growth and income growth. Now we're getting that." Still, the recovery has a long way to go to compensate for the roughly 8 million jobs lost in the United States since the onset of the recession, and some experts predict that with the depressed housing market, many good-paying construction jobs and other positions that relate to the home-building field will not make a comeback any time soon. In fact, on June 4, 2010, the *New York Times* reported that most new jobs in the past month were created by the federal government to aid in amassing the Census data—and these will be temporary positions. Several economists caution that the country needs to create 100,000 to 130,000 jobs each month just to keep up with new workers entering the market. Only the creation of employment opportunities above those figures will start putting those who lost their jobs back to work.

Psychologists and other mental health experts worry that without the prospect of such massive job creation, long-term unemployment may negatively impact families and have devastating effects that go beyond financial loss. Depression, anxiety, and loss of self-esteem are common problems for unemployed workers. Suicide rates generally rise during periods of high unemployment, and even those who are not disposed to such rash acts often try to dull their fears with alcohol and drug use. Battling depression or simply bickering over money problems can also strain familial relationships. In a February 2009 CNBC web article, financial correspondent Sharon Epperson cautioned that "studies show that when a spouse is laid off, a couple is more likely to divorce within a year than those who are both married and employed." Children may also be affected by the emotional strain placed on families coping with unemployment.

Though much of the news about the continuing recession remains grim, many analysts are confident that the worst is over. President Obama has averred that despite the controversy surrounding the stimulus, the crisis would have deepened without the infusion of tax dollars. "We are beginning to turn the corner," the president said in April 2010. "This month, more Americans woke up, got dressed and headed to work at an office or factory or storefront." Indeed, some economists are pleased that the economy is making headway—and some have commented that, of all the job growth figures cited by various polls, the most promising are those that reveal growth in manufacturing—the industry that has been decimated by the crisis as well as by years of sending these jobs off-shore to foreign countries with cheaper labor. In April 2010, Timothy R. Homan reported on the *Bloomberg Businessweek* website that "manufacturers so far this year have added 45,000 workers to payrolls, the biggest three-month gain in the industry since March–May 2004." Such unexpected news heartens some observers and may be a justifiable cause for optimism. However, recovery will not be quick, and most Americans acknowledge that fact. According to an April 2010 Gallup poll, 55 percent of Americans believe the recovery will not start for another two or more years.

In *Opposing Viewpoints: Unemployment*, various political, media, and business experts explain their views on the state of the recession and the impact of joblessness on the United States. In four chapters—What Contributes to Unemployment? Who Is Particularly Affected by High Unemployment? How Effective Is the Government's Response to Unemployment? and What Can Policy Makers and Businesses Do to Reduce Unemployment?—these analysts confront the reality of high unemployment and debate the best remedies to put the nation back on its feet. Some fear American unemployment may never return to its pre-crisis rate; others place their trust in the country's work ethic and the resilience of the market. Meanwhile, millions of Americans continue to struggle day-to-day to make ends meet while looking for work in an economy that seems so alien to those who held jobs during the pre-crisis years of high consumer spending, relative stock stability, and a 5 percent national unemployment rate.

What Contributes to Unemployment?

Chapter Preface

Business analysts understand that unemployment is a natural part of a healthy economy. It is unlikely, for example, that all workers will be continuously employed as their lives change. Some might be dissatisfied with their jobs and quit before acquiring a new position; others might be forced to relocate and thus exist without a job for several months. These contingencies make up what economists call frictional unemployment. Structural unemployment, on the other hand, denotes market changes that make certain positions superfluous, thus forcing people into unemployment or making their job training useless. Thus, technological advances or the outsourcing of jobs to cheaper locations typically brings about layoffs as workers' skills are no longer needed. Similarly, if jobs in certain fields are not in high demand, competition to enter those fields will ensure that some of the workers who trained to enter those markets will not find employment. Some economists believe that structural unemployment is the price a country pays to innovate and maintain an edge in the global marketplace.

Frictional and structural unemployment are natural—and even tolerable—because they stem from changes in the labor market. That is, workers are either in transition or in need of new skills. The more worrisome form of unemployment arises from the business sector. Cyclical unemployment describes the lack of jobs that occurs from changes in industry demand. When business production is near maximum, cyclical unemployment will be low; when the demand for certain products drops, then cyclical unemployment will rise. Many economists assert that the high unemployment rate that resulted from the 2008 financial crisis is a byproduct of low industrial production. With loss of capital and fear of the unstable market, companies are unable to create jobs and therefore cannot work at peak production. Writing for the Heritage Foundation on March 24, 2010, senior policy analyst James Sherk contends, "It is the sharp drop in creation of new jobs that explains the severity of this recession. The credit crunch, the collapse of the housing bubble, and harmful economic policies have made the economy less hospitable to entrepreneurs. This bad business climate discourages business owners from expanding." Until businesses believe consumer confidence has returned and the investment climate has stabilized, they will not create the jobs needed to reduce the nation's unemployment level.

Author and entrepreneur Martin Ford claims that cyclical unemployment is being driven by structural changes. In his view, business leaders are taking advantage of the bad economy to eliminate positions that have for years been obviated by technology and outsourcing. In a May 24, 2010, piece for the *Huffington Post*, Ford resists the notion that rising production will decrease unemployment. As he writes, "Many mainstream economists are projecting that unemployment will remain high for years to come—but there is a near universal expectation that eventually, the problem will correct itself and we will gravitate back to something close to full employment. The problem with this assumption is that technology is not going to stop advancing while we are all waiting for the job market to recover." Ford maintains that as businesses find cheaper ways of replacing human workers, they will not seek to create more positions because to do so would unnecessarily cut into profits. Ford and the other five analysts in the following chapter debate some of the commonly proposed reasons why unemployment has remained so high in the United States during the past few years.

Viewpoint 1

"International trade agreements are not designed to benefit the United States, its people, its workers, or its future."

Globalization Increases U.S. Unemployment

Darren Weeks

In the following viewpoint, Darren Weeks claims that America's pro-globalization policies are responsible for widespread unemployment in America. According to Weeks, economic treaties such as the North American Free Trade Agreement are a means for U.S. businesses to outsource jobs to nations where labor is cheap while laying off millions of better-paid Americans. He insists that globalization has not brought jobs to the United States but has instead destroyed U.S. manufacturing and lowered the standard of living of all working Americans. Weeks is the host of the "Govern America" talk and news show on the Republic Broadcasting Network, a radio and Internet operation.

As you read, consider the following questions:

1. How many jobs did U.S. companies cut in July 2009, according to Weeks?

Darren Weeks, "Unemployment: Now, That's Sustainable!" NewsWithViews.com, October 18, 2009. http://newswithviews.com. Reproduced by permission.

2. What was the last year that the United States enjoyed a trade surplus with Mexico, as Weeks reports?
3. Whom does Weeks blame for instituting the President's Council on Sustainable Development that, in Weeks's view, helped redistribute America's wealth to developing countries?

Every time the media reports the unemployment numbers, it reminds me of George Orwell's book, *1984*. In the legendary book, a governmental organization referred to as the "Ministry of Truth" would report through the telescreens that the price of chocolate was going down. Winston Smith, the lead character of the book, knew good and well that the price of chocolate was not going down but was actually going up. We are certainly living in Orwell's world! The difference between ours and the fictional world of Orwell, is that we are not being propagandized about chocolate, but rather unemployment statistics. The controlled news media always attempts to "butter up" the bad numbers, by putting a positive spin on the fact that we are losing our jobs, month after month.

The truth of the matter is that America is in deep, deep trouble and all the gutless globalist lapdogs in the media can do is lie to the people, trying to convince them that we are not in a depression—it's only a "recession"—and it will soon be over. The deception is intended to get the American people, true to the failed Keynesian economic model,[1] to spend money they don't have, in a hopeless attempt to apply the defibrillation paddles to the dying patient which is the American economy. They will never tell you the patient is dying. They will never tell you *why* the patient is dying.

1. Keynesian economics promotes a mixed economy, where the government and public sector have the power to influence the private business sector in order to create stability.

Furthermore, I have to laugh when I read statements like those of Don Miller from *Money Morning* when he said in a recent column about the horrendous September [2009] unemployment numbers,

> "The latest data suggest the odds are increasing that the economy may be suffering through its second 'jobless recovery' in eight years."

I have news for Don and all of the people in the media and elsewhere who still have their heads in the sand about what is really going on in America. Listen up! Hear me! There isn't going to be a recovery! You cannot have a recovery without jobs! And you are never going to see our jobs return without a reversal of the policies of globalization which put America into this economic mess.

No End to American Job Loss

It isn't difficult to see the devastation that the policies which gave us the "global economy" have wrought upon America and her people. American companies cut 371,000 jobs in July [2009]. Not surprisingly, August wasn't much better. Mike Larsen at *Money and Markets* puts it this way,

> "In the week ending August 29: 570,000 Americans filed for first-time jobless benefits. The number of Americans who had previously filed and still remain on the jobless rolls was 6.234 million.
>
> "While those numbers are down somewhat from their March highs, they're far, far above what would be considered normal. The average reading for initial claims over the past 42 years is just under 360,000.
>
> "Then there's this week's report from ADP Employer Services. It showed the economy shedding another 298,000 jobs in August. While that was down from 360,000 a month earlier, it also marked the 19th straight month we've lost jobs as a nation. The cumulative tally: Almost 6.9 million jobs down the drain!"

September's numbers are not much better. Reuters news service recently reported that U.S. employers cut another 260,000 jobs last month. Hence, building on Larsen's numbers, we've now gone 20 straight months with a hemorrhaging U.S. job market and there's no end in sight.

These are astronomical numbers! Add this figure to the already overwhelming number of job losses that we've seen since the signing of the NAFTA, [North American Free Trade Agreement] agreement in 1993, and it doesn't take a rocket scientist (or an economist, for that matter) to see the effects of globalization upon our country. Yet, do we see any sign of reversal of those same policies? Quite the contrary.

In fact, anyone arguing for a common sense rescission of WTO [World Trade Organization] agreements, a return of our military to our own soil, and an end to the flood of migrant workers coming to this country, is referred to with such disdainful pejoratives as "isolationist," "protectionist," and even "xenophobic."

Denying the Problem

A perfect example of the mindset of out-of-touch elitism that has permeated globalist circles can be seen in the *Foreign Affairs* article titled, "The Outsourcing Bogeyman" by Daniel Drezner, assistant political science professor at the University of Chicago. Drezner pontificated in his May 2004 article,

> "Should Americans be concerned about the economic effects of outsourcing? Not particularly. . . . The creation of new jobs overseas will eventually lead to more jobs and higher incomes in the United States. Because the economy—and especially job growth—is sluggish at the moment, commentators are attempting to draw a connection between offshore outsourcing and high unemployment. But believing that offshore outsourcing causes unemployment is the economic equivalent of believing the sun revolves around the earth: intuitively compelling but clearly wrong."

What elitist arrogance! And what an insult to the intelligence of the average, every day American workers—who, by the hundreds of thousands, have watched their factories close and their jobs disappear to foreign countries in the post-NAFTA economy! I would like to say to Mr. Drezner that denial is not a river in Egypt. Why don't you spend some of your millions and take a trip to Motown [Detroit, Michigan] and tell your philosophy to the unemployed auto workers there? Why don't you come down from your ivory tower to Main Street America where the armed guards are posted at the grocery stores and where tent cities permeate the landscape?

Mr. Drezner concludes,

> "Until robust job growth returns, the debate over outsourcing will not go away—the political temptation to scapegoat foreigners is simply too great.
>
> "The refrain of 'this time, it's different' is not new in the debate over free trade. In the 1980's, the Japanese variety of capitalism—with its omniscient industrial policy and high nontariff barriers—was supposed to supplant the U.S. system. Fifteen years later, that prediction sounds absurd. During the 1990's, the passage of NAFTA and the Uruguay Round of trade talks were supposed to create a 'giant sucking sound' as jobs left the United States. Contrary to such fears, tens of millions of new jobs were created. Once the economy improves, the political hysteria over outsourcing will also disappear."

Tens of millions of new jobs were created since NAFTA? Where are they, Mr. Drezner? Perhaps in government think tanks and academic egg heads who've never gotten their carefully-manicured hands dirty because they've never done a real day's work in their entire lives?

The Need for Trade Policies That Stop Giving Advantages to Foreign Countries

[The United States needs to enact] complementary trade policies that prevent other economies from gaining unfair competitive advantages. The trade deficits accumulated during the [George W.] Bush administration—a whopping $4.8 trillion—were a major cause of the loss overseas of 5.3 million manufacturing jobs and more than 2 million service jobs; and they made the economy about $1.5 trillion smaller than it would otherwise have been. We couldn't afford these economy-zapping job losses then, and we certainly can't afford them now.

Leo Hindery Jr. and Leo W. Gerard,
"Our Jobless Recovery," Nation, *July 13, 2009.*

Free Trade Agreements That Do Not Benefit America

Let's talk for a moment about that "giant sucking sound" that [business leader and former presidential candidate] Ross Perot predicted and that globalist/elitist Drezner likes to discount. Several months ago, your writer personally pulled the official NAFTA trade deficit numbers directly off the U.S. Census Bureau web site. These are the official numbers, according to the government's own statisticians.

In the years preceding the signing of the NAFTA agreement, the U.S. trade deficit hovered around even with Mexico give or take a billion or two. In 1991, the U.S. enjoyed a $2.1 billion trade surplus, meaning we exported more dollars worth of goods to Mexico than we imported. In 1992, that number was over $5.3 billion. In 1993, the year NAFTA was signed,

American workers enjoyed a $1.6 billion trade surplus. The following year, the effects of NAFTA hadn't yet hit the American economy. The U.S. still experienced a $1.3 billion surplus. However, that was the last year for any surplus.

By 1995, just two years after the passage of NAFTA, the U.S. economy began feeling the effects in a major way. We went from having a $1.3 billion trade surplus in 1994, to having a $15.8 billion trade deficit the following year, and the figure has climbed almost without exception every year. By 2007, the U.S. trade deficit with Mexico was a staggering $74.6 billion. It's important to note that NAFTA is only one trade agreement. There are several such agreements that our government has made with impoverished countries, including the Central American Free Trade Agreement [CAFTA], passed by the U.S. Senate on June 30, 2005 and signed by George W. Bush on August 2nd of the same year.

As I pointed out in my May 9, 2005 blog entry, "CAFTA: Opening foreign markets? What markets?," nearly every one of the countries covered by the CAFTA-DR [Dominican Republic–Central America–United States Free Trade Agreement] agreement are highly impoverished, according to the *CIA World Fact Book*. Here's the brief rundown:

- Guatemala—Over 75% of the population lives below the poverty line.
- Honduras—"one of the poorest countries in the Western Hemisphere."
- El Salvador—"GDP [gross domestic product] per capita is roughly half that of Brazil, Argentina, and Chile . . . With the adoption of the US dollar as its currency, El Salvador has lost control over monetary policy and must concentrate on maintaining a disciplined fiscal policy."

- Nicaragua—"Nicaragua, one of the hemisphere's poorest countries, faces low per capita income, massive unemployment, and huge external debt . . . Nicaragua qualified in early 2004 for some $4 billion in foreign debt reduction under the Heavily Indebted Poor Countries (HIPC) initiative." Half the population lives beneath the poverty line.
- Costa Rica—Fairs better than the rest, the wealthiest of these countries. The only Central American country where citizens are not leaving in search of opportunities.
- Dominican Republic—1 out of every 4 live in poverty.

As I asked back in 2005, I again press for an answer: Given the dire condition of these nations' economies, how could "President" George W. Bush make the case that having a free trade agreement with these impoverished Central American countries be in the best interest of American citizens and workers? How could American exporters—what's left of them—expect to gain from a market where the people are too impoverished to buy? The truth of the matter is that they haven't, and they won't.

Lowering U.S. Standard of Living to Third-World Levels

Mr. Drezner's chief problem, along with other Establishment elitists like him, is that he has selective statistics. Those he would call "protectionists" also have statistics. The real difference is that while the statistics produced by Drezner's ilk are produced in the academic meat grinder to be vomited out in globalist publications, ours is backed by indisputable reality—knowing that the average American doesn't need academic, media, or government statisticians telling them how good they have it. The numbers the American people look at are their bank accounts, their credit scores, their mortgage payments, their heating and grocery bills, and the price of gas. Increasingly, despite Mr. Drezner's high rhetoric, Americans have been looking at the digits on their unemployment checks.

The only logical conclusion is that international trade agreements are not designed to benefit the United States, its people, its workers, or its future. They are designed to benefit the poorest countries, at the expense of the American people, leveling the "playing field", lowering the American standard of living down to the "sustainable" level of third-world status. In other words, unemployment in America, the loss of our jobs, the shrinking of the American way of life, the eradication of our freedom to travel, the elimination of the middle class is socially and environmentally "sustainable." The wealth of the American people is to be redistributed to the poorest nations, in accordance with chapter 3 of Agenda 21 [a United Nations resolution on sustainable development passed in 1992]. Our consumption patterns have to be changed in accordance with chapter 4 of Agenda 21. We've been sold out by globalist scum, and nothing is ever going to change unless the people understand that this is a part of a deliberate agenda. It isn't incompetence on the part of our "elected" officials. It isn't a recession. It isn't a bad economic downturn. It's the effects of globalism. Period! We are reaping the natural results of policies that are designed to bankrupt our country.

Pro-Globalization Politicians Are Traitors

I hear people say, all of the time, regarding the economy, "it will come back." Sorry to burst your bubble, but no it won't! It will never come back until the WTO trade agreements which put us into this mess are rescinded. That won't happen until the appropriate pressure is applied to Washington by the people and by our state lawmakers who must be pressured to go to Washington and demand the changes.

And if you people who call yourselves "Democrats," think your buddy [President Barack] Obama is any better than Bush was, then I ask why hasn't he rescinded these treaties which have obviously been so detrimental to our country? Why haven't the unions—which have seen their memberships and dues decline—demanded a revoking of the international trade agreements that have brought America to its knees? Keep in mind, it was the unions which helped put [President Bill] Clinton in office, who then stabbed the American worker in the back by promoting NAFTA after promising to oppose it. It was Bill Clinton who established the President's Council on Sustainable Development to kick start Agenda 21 implementation in the United States after the 1992 Rio Earth Summit. Agenda 21 implementation mandates the redistribution of wealth from developed to developing countries. It is the reason why your jobs have left. It is Bill's wife, [Secretary of State] Hillary Clinton, who currently serves as head of the U.S. State Department, which is the chief agency of the United States government that implements the UN [United Nations] agenda of "sustainability" in America.

When will the American people ever realize that there is no difference between parties? We are not red states, blue states, conservatives, liberals, Republicans, or Democrats. We are Americans. It is about time we dispelled with the labels that the social engineers have developed to divide us—and that we've so freely embraced for ourselves—and began to act like true countrymen.

An ancient Roman philosopher named Cicero once said, "A nation can survive its fools, and even the ambitious. But it cannot survive treason from within. An enemy at the gates is less formidable, for he is known and he carries his banners openly against the city. But the traitor moves among those within the gates freely, his sly whispers rustling through all the alleys, heard in the very halls of government itself. For the traitor appears no traitor; he speaks in the accents familiar to his victims, and he wears their face and their garments, and he appeals to the baseness that lies deep in the hearts of all men. He rots the soul of a nation; he works secretly and unknown in the night to undermine the pillars of a city; he infects the body politic so that it can no longer resist. A murderer is less to be feared."

Surrendering Sovereignty to Globalists

As I write these words [October 2009], Ireland has just voted for a second time on the Lisbon Treaty, the Constitution of the European Union [EU]. Unlike the first time where they voted it down last year, they just approved it by a margin of 67 to 33 percent. Their government's fear campaign of economic doom and gloom was the chief reason for the voters who favored it at the polls, according to exit polls. In other words, they were willing to hand the sovereignty of their country over to a regional governing body on the promise of economic prosperity.

They bought the same globalist lie for which America fell when we accepted GATT [General Agreement on Tariffs and Trade], NAFTA, CAFTA and many other foreign trade entanglements. If Poland and the Czech Republic follow Ireland—and they are expected to do so—we can look forward to a new European presidency and Secretary of State to be formed. Ireland will eventually cease to exist, as the sovereignty of all of the 27 member countries of the EU will be gradually chipped away, until there is nothing left.

As Americans tail gate, drink beer, and watch their football games, they don't have time to worry about the fate of the Irish, the Poles, or the Czechs. But they would do well to learn the lessons of Europe. As the globalist thieves have taken Ireland, so too they come for the west.

> *"The protectionists' proposed policies would sharply increase the agony of unemployment."*

Globalization's Negative Impact on U.S. Unemployment Is Exaggerated

Part I: William H. Overholt; Part II: Daniel Griswold

In the following viewpoint, William H. Overholt and Daniel Griswold conclude that many observers who have watched America lose jobs in recent years have unjustly blamed U.S. globalization policies for mining the economy. In part I of the viewpoint, Overholt, the director of the Center for Asia Pacific Policy at the RAND Corporation, maintains that free trade has slowly increased the average wages of workers even as jobs have fled the country. Overholt claims that free trade policies have actually saved many jobs in the United States, and he asserts that once America's economy adjusts to globalization, other job opportunities will grow. In part II of the viewpoint, Daniel Griswold, the director of the Center for Trade Policy Studies at the libertarian Cato Institute, defends globalization's benefits as well. According to Griswold, the current economic crisis that has put many people out of work was caused by fiscal and housing policies, not by trade liberalization. Griswold argues that globalization has created jobs in America, especially among export businesses and other industries that can now sell to open markets around the world. He also insists that while America is losing some of its manufacturing base, the nation is creating more, good-paying jobs in service fields such as education, health care, and business.

As you read, consider the following questions:

1. According to Overholt, what is the principle cause of job loss in the United States?
2. In Overholt's opinion, why does France have such a high unemployment rate?
3. What is the fourth largest export market for U.S. goods, according to Griswold?

Protectionists who characterize free trade as almost treasonous are on a crusade to build new barriers around America in an effort to keep jobs in and imports out.

Some have built careers around denouncing the evils of globalization. CNN commentator Lou Dobbs, for example, criticizes free trade on a regular basis on his nightly show and in his book *Exporting America: Why Corporate Greed is Shipping American Jobs Overseas.* A promo for the book on the CNN Web site states: "The shipment of American jobs to cheap foreign labor markets threatens not only millions of workers and their families, but also the American way of life."

The most serious critique of globalization is the charge that it promotes inequality, driving down U.S. wages while enriching millionaire corporate executives. This charge is partly true, but mostly false.

Expanding the Global Workforce

The true part is that within many countries, globalization has enhanced the wealth of business owners and managers while providing proportionately less wage growth for ordinary workers. It has done so by expanding the workforce participating in the modern world economy to include much of the populations of Eastern Europe, China and India.

As a result, millions of workers in the U.S. and Western Europe now face more competition than ever before from others willing to work for far lower wages. Capital has not experienced a proportionate increase in competition, so the share of corporate profits has risen and the share of wages has fallen. The rich get richer, while incomes of workers as a whole go up as well, but more slowly.

Some manufacturing workers in the United States—such as those who labored in huge factories making basic steel—have suffered as they've seen their jobs leave America for low-wage countries. But for workers as a whole, the truth about globalization and inequality is the opposite of what the protectionists claim. There are three caveats to the steel worker's story and two larger perspectives on inequality.

Increased Productivity Displaces Workers

One caveat is that protectionists enormously exaggerate the negative effects of globalization by attributing virtually all manufacturing job losses to competition with China. We are told by union leaders and some politicians that America is exporting millions of jobs to China. This is absolutely untrue.

Scholarly studies show that most job losses in the United States are attributable to domestic causes such as increased domestic productivity. A few years ago it took 40 hours of labor to produce a car. Now it takes 15. That translates into a need for fewer workers. Protectionists who blame China for such job losses are being intellectually dishonest. In fact, both China and the U.S. have lost manufacturing jobs due to rising productivity, but China has lost ten times more—a decline of about 25 million Chinese jobs from over 54 million in 1994 to under 30 million ten years later.

A second caveat is that there are two ways to increase people's standard of living. One is to increase their wages. The other is to decrease prices so that they can buy more things with the same amount of money.

The ability to buy inexpensive, quality Chinese-made shoes and Japanese-made cars at lower prices disproportionately benefits lower income Americans. The Wall Street banker who pays $350 for Church's shoes benefits relatively little, but the janitor who buys shoes for $25 rather than $50 at Payless or Target or Wal-Mart benefits greatly.

Lower prices due to imports from China alone—ignoring all other similar results of globalization—probably raise the real incomes of lower income Americans by 5 to 10 percent. That's something no welfare program has ever accomplished.

Globalization Saves Jobs

A third caveat is that the protectionists never mention the jobs created and saved by globalization. If General Motors avoids bankruptcy, as seems likely, one important reason will be the profits it has made by selling cars in China. The vast China market, and the ability of American corporations to expand and refine their operations through a division of labor with China, creates many high level jobs in U.S. operations ranging in diversity from Motorola to IBM to Caterpillar to Boeing to farming.

The first of the larger perspectives on globalization is that open economies adjust faster to their real competitive advantages, allowing them to employ their own people. The most recent U.S. unemployment rate, [in 2006] was 4.4 percent. France, along with other relatively protected economies, typically has twice as high a proportion of the population unemployed because their workers are stuck in inappropriate jobs.

Still more protected economies, like many in Latin America, often run much higher rates of unemployment—up to 40%. Economies more open than the U.S.—like Singapore and Hong Kong—historically run lower rates of unemployment.

The worst inequality is between families whose breadwinners have jobs and those who don't. Globalization minimizes that problem.

Bringing Millions out of Poverty

Globalization has brought countries with about 3 billion people from subhuman conditions of life into modern standards of living with adequate food, basic shelter, modern clothing rather than rags, and life spans that are over 60 rather than under 45. (In the early 1950s, China's life expectancy was 41 years, in 2005 it was 72.7 years.) This is the greatest reduction of inequality that has happened in human history.

In East Asia, this reduction of inequality has resulted from a wave of economic growth that has swept through Japan, Taiwan, South Korea, Thailand, Malaysia, and much of Indonesia. It is rapidly spreading across China, is well on the way in India and Vietnam and is coming to other countries around the world.

The world's fastest growth is occurring in some of its poorest countries, notably India, China and Indonesia. The middle income countries are growing faster on average than the rich countries. In other words, global inequality is declining fast.

It is not surprising when workers in industries undergoing adjustment complain about the pain of change. For many families, prolonged unemployment can wipe out their savings, cost them their homes and turn their lives into a nightmare. The suffering of these families can't be ignored.

But sound economics is based on facts grounded in objective analysis, not on emotion. Sometimes, what seems like a "common sense" solution is not really very sensible at all, as is seen with the arguments of the protectionists. Even the best of intentions can, in the end, bring about the worst of outcomes. The protectionists' proposed policies would sharply increase the agony of unemployment.

America will not benefit if an increasing number of opinion leaders and elected officials use exaggerated, partial views of inequality to try to lead us into a future of slower growth, higher unemployment and greater world tensions.

Instead, America and its leaders should focus on how the nation can use the rapidly expanding economy to assist individuals who have suffered from globalization to get the education, training and opportunities in new industries they need to benefit rather than suffer from globalization.

Part II

Tune in to cable TV, talk radio, or the blogosphere and you will soon be hit over the head with the message that free trade is destroying America. According to the economic populists on the left and right, imports and outsourcing threaten the wages, jobs, and futures of Main Street Americans.

On trade, as on so much else, the populists have it wrong again. Free trade and globalization are great blessings to families across America.

Now [March 2010] may seem an odd moment to tout the benefits of trade. After all, unemployment is 10 percent and housing and manufacturing remain in a slump. The Great Recession of 2008–09 [the longest economic downturn in the U.S. of the post-World War II era, officially lasting from December 2007 to June 2009] was not caused by trade, however, but by misguided monetary and housing policies that were "Made in the USA."

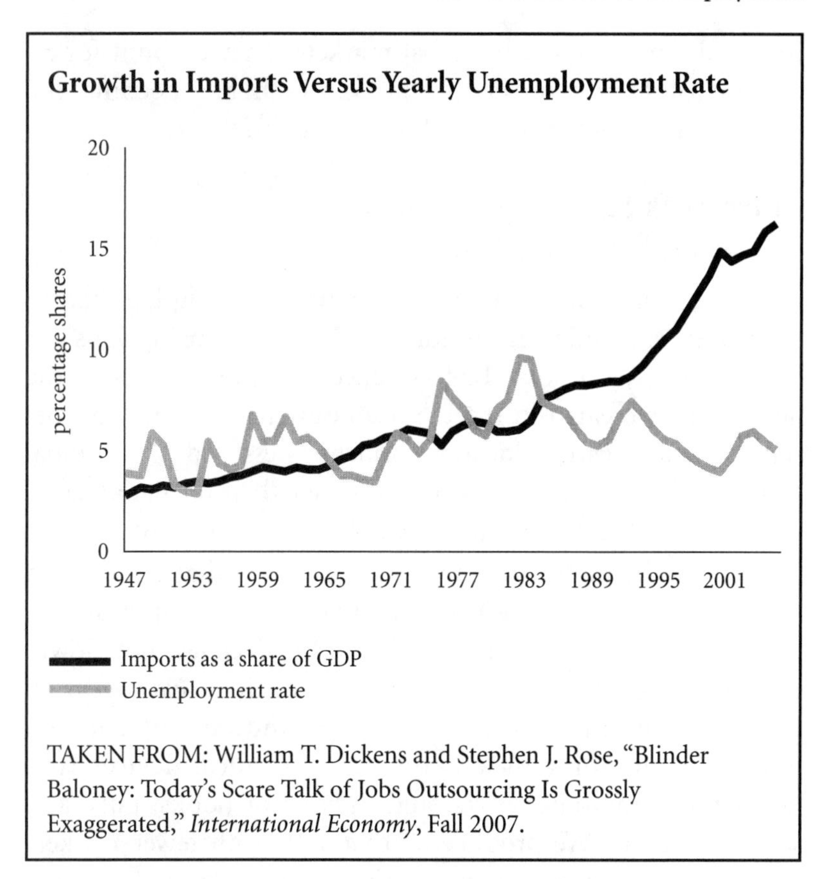

Growth in Imports Versus Yearly Unemployment Rate

TAKEN FROM: William T. Dickens and Stephen J. Rose, "Blinder Baloney: Today's Scare Talk of Jobs Outsourcing Is Grossly Exaggerated," *International Economy*, Fall 2007.

Exporting to Global Markets

During difficult economic times, import competition allows more American families to keep their heads above water by delivering lower prices on staples such as food, clothing, and shoes. The prices we pay for goods exposed to global trade tend to rise more slowly than inflation or even fall. The imported fresh fruits and vegetables, T-shirts and discounted sneakers sold at big-box retailers are especially important in the budgets of poor and middle-class families.

Trade allows Americans to sell our goods and services in growing markets abroad. Exporting is not just a Fortune 500 phenomenon. With the help of the Internet and shippers such as FedEx, a quarter of a million small and medium-sized U.S.

companies now export to global markets. They account for 30 percent of U.S. exports to China, which has become the fourth-largest foreign market for U.S. goods.

America Is Still Creating Jobs and Manufacturing Goods

For Americans worried about their jobs, it is a Big Lie that we have been surrendering middle-class manufacturing jobs for low-paying service jobs. In fact, since 1991, two-thirds of the net new jobs created in the U.S. economy have been in sectors such as health care, education, and business and professional services where the average wage is higher than in manufacturing. America today is a middle-class service economy.

Yet another myth of the trade debate is that America is "deindustrializing." In fact, the total volume of output at U.S. factories has been trending up in recent decades, not down. American workers on American soil continue each year to produce thousands of civilian aircraft and aircraft engines, millions of motor vehicles, computers, medical devices, and heavy household appliances, and billions of books, pills, and semiconductors. We produce all that stuff with fewer workers because our manufacturing workers have become so much more productive.

Beyond our borders, the past three decades of expanding trade and globalization have witnessed dramatic global progress. Between 1981 and 2005, the share of the world's population living on the equivalent of $1.25 a day dropped by half, from 52 to 25 percent, according to the World Bank.

As a global middle class has emerged, so too have more democratic forms of government. The share of the world's population living in countries that respect civil liberties and the right to vote has climbed from 35 percent in 1973 to 46 percent today, according to [international organization] Freedom House. And fewer people are dying in wars today than in past decades, in large part because commerce has replaced military competition.

America and the world face daunting tasks today, as in generations past, but expanding trade is part of the solution, not part of the problem.

VIEWPOINT 

> *"Technological progress is relentless, and machines and computers will eventually approach the point where they will match or exceed the average worker's ability to perform most routine work tasks."*

Technology and Automation Increase Unemployment

Martin Ford

In the following viewpoint, Martin Ford argues that advances in artificial intelligence and robots will increasingly allow computers to do the jobs of people. He predicts that the reliability and precision of these technological workers will compel business owners to adopt them or lose their competitive edge. Ford also predicts that the large number of displaced humans will never be reemployed because he believes most industries will convert to automated workforces. Ford is a computer designer and the founder of a software firm. He also is the author of The Lights in the Tunnel: Automation, Accelerating Technology and the Economy of the Future.

As you read, consider the following questions:

1. According to Ford, college-educated job seekers will eventually be threatened by what two competitors?
2. Why does Ford believe automation is capable of displacing a very large percentage of the 140 million workers in the United States?
3. Why does Ford predict the "business models of mass market industries would be threatened" by rampant automation?

The official unemployment rate remains at 10% [in January 2010], and economists are projecting that the job market will take years to recover. Is it possible that, beyond the obvious impact of the financial crisis, there is another largely unacknowledged factor contributing significantly to the dismal unemployment situation?

I believe that there is, and I argue that case in my new book, *The Lights in the Tunnel: Automation, Accelerating Technology and the Economy of the Future*. In the past two decades, information technology has advanced dramatically and is increasingly being employed to eliminate jobs of all types. Job automation technology, together with globalization, has been the primary force behind the stagnant wages and diminished opportunities for less educated workers we've seen in recent years.

Robots Replacing Human Workers

Because information technology accelerates (roughly doubling every two years), rather than increasing at a constant rate, we can expect that the coming years and decades will see even more dramatic progress. In the future, automation is no longer going to be something that primarily impacts low wage, uneducated workers. Technologies such as artificial intelligence, machine learning and software automation applications will increasingly enable computers to do jobs that require significant training and education. College graduates who take "knowledge worker" jobs will find themselves threatened not only by low-wage offshore competitors but also by machines and software algorithms that can perform sophisticated analysis and decision making.

At the same time, continuing progress in manufacturing automation and the introduction of advanced commercial robots will continue to diminish opportunities for lower skill workers. Technological progress is relentless, and machines and computers will eventually approach the point where they will match or exceed the average worker's ability to perform most routine work tasks. The result is likely to be structural unemployment that ultimately impacts the workforce at virtually all levels—from workers without high school diplomas to those who hold graduate degrees.

The Economy Cannot Absorb Millions of Displaced Workers

Most mainstream economists dismiss this scenario. They continue to believe that the economy will restructure and create adequate numbers of jobs in the long run. Historically this has, in fact, been the case. Millions of jobs were eliminated in agriculture when mechanized farm equipment was introduced. That resulted in a migration to the manufacturing sector. Likewise, manufacturing automation and globalization has resulted in the transition to a largely service-based economy in the United States and other developed countries.

In the past, technology has typically impacted one employment sector at a time, leaving or creating other areas for workers to transition into. That's unlikely to be the case this time around. Accelerating information technology will offer a completely unprecedented level of work capability—and it can be applied virtually everywhere. As technology providers compete and innovate, automation will certainly become more af-

Losing Jobs to Robots

As CPU [Central Processing Unit] chips and memory systems finally reach parity with the human brain, and then surpass it, robots will be able to perform nearly any normal job that a human performs today. The self-service checkout lines that are springing up everywhere are the first sign of the trend. . . .

The problem, of course, is that all of these robots will eliminate a huge portion of the jobs currently held by human beings. For example, there are 3.5 million jobs in the fast food industry alone. Many of those will be lost to kiosks. Many more will be lost to robots that can flip burgers and clean bathrooms. Eventually they will all be lost. The only people who will still have jobs in the fast food industry will be the senior management team at corporate headquarters.

The same sort of thing will happen in retail stores, hotels, airports, factories, construction sites, delivery companies and so on. All of these jobs will evaporate at approximately the same time, leaving all of those workers unemployed. The Post Office, FedEx and UPS together employed over a million workers in 2002. Once robots can drive the trucks and deliver the packages at a much lower cost than human workers can, those 1,000,000 or so employees will be out on the street.

Marshall Brain, "Robotic Nation," MarshallBrain.com, 2008. http://marshallbrain.com.

fordable and more accessible to even the smallest businesses. If a business can save money through automation, competitive pressures will leave it no choice but to do so. While there will certainly continue to be jobs that cannot be automated, the reality is that a very large percentage of the 140 million or so workers in the United States are employed in jobs that are fundamentally routine and repetitive in nature. Enormous numbers of these jobs are going to be vaporized by technology in the coming decades, and because that technology will be available across the board, there is really very little reason to believe that entirely new employment sectors capable of absorbing massive numbers of workers will be created.

The Looming Financial Crisis

The problem is not just one of unemployment. In my book, I use a thought experiment or mental simulation based on "lights in a tunnel" to illustrate the overall economic impact of relentlessly advancing job automation technology. As unemployment increases and wages fall, discretionary consumer spending and confidence will likewise plummet. The result will be a downward economic spiral that will be very difficult to arrest. Beyond some threshold, the business models of mass market industries would be threatened as there would simply be too few viable consumers to purchase their products. We would also likely see unprecedented levels of debt defaults, plunging asset values and financial system disruptions that might easily exceed what has so far occurred in the current crisis.

I believe that the impact of accelerating automation technology is likely to present an enormous economic, social and political challenge over the next ten to twenty years and beyond. Yet, the issue is simply not on the radar. In *The Lights in the Tunnel* I suggest some possible reforms that might address the issue, but the reality is that the problem is potentially so disruptive that even progressive thinkers would probably find some of my ideas extreme. Conservatives will likely view my proposals as unthinkable. Nonetheless, if we are ultimately destined to progress into a world where traditional jobs are simply unavailable and where a huge percentage of the population has little in the way of marketable skills or opportunity to earn an income, there will be few if any viable solutions that would not be perceived as radical.

> *"U.S. technology and business innovators recognize that robots in factories have the potential to save and create more jobs than they eliminate."*

Technology and Automation Create Jobs

Jeff Burnstein

In the viewpoint that follows, Jeff Burnstein tries to calm fears that technological innovations will lead to widespread human unemployment. He insists that robotics and other automation fields allow businesses to remain competitive, dispensing with dangerous and repetitive jobs and replacing those with higher-paying, skilled jobs. Burnstein also contends that various industries related to automation—such as robotics and machine repair—will likely see a gain in employment as more companies demand these services. Burnstein is the president of the Robotic Industries Association, a Michigan-based trade group that promotes the use of robotics in industry.

As you read, consider the following questions:

1. What new industries does Burnstein say will need robots and thus give a boost to robotics industries?

Jeff Burnstein, "Robots Can Create Jobs, Too," Robotic Industries Association, June 1, 2010.

2. According to the author, in what year was the first industrial robot installed?
3. About how many robots are operating in businesses worldwide, according to Burnstein?

Industrial robots can help companies compete by boosting quality and productivity. That's ultimately a benefit for American labor.

If you work in an American manufacturing company today [2010], you should be worried about your job. I live in Michigan and have witnessed the destruction caused by shuttered factories and jobs shipped overseas. When plants close, whole communities suffer.

With unemployment at about 14 percent or higher in Michigan, it's not surprising some workers are afraid of robots capable of working seven days a week, 24 hours a day with great accuracy and reliability, capable of performing many tasks better than people.

Automation Makes Businesses More Competitive

That fear, so prevalent in the early days of robotics, today is misplaced. What should really give workers pause is when their companies won't use robots and other automated technologies to become stronger global competitors.

U.S. technology and business innovators recognize that robots in factories have the potential to save and create more jobs than they eliminate. Robots help companies turn out higher-quality and lower-cost goods to compete with those made in China, Mexico, India, or other low-wage nations. They remove people from dangerous and boring jobs they shouldn't have been doing in the first place, and put them in higher-skilled, higher-paying positions.

Stimulating Job Growth

There's also a large ecosystem of robotics-related companies in America that employ thousands of people who design, build, program, and service robots and the equipment they work with.

Look at the some of the new industries America wants to develop. To get the desired quality and productivity from plants that produce wind turbines, solar panels, and advanced batteries and the cars they go in, we need robots. They're just as essential to the successful development of these industries as they are to aerospace, consumer packaged goods, electronics, food, and lab automation.

Look at the new General Motors [GM], whose Buick LaCrosse is built in its Fairfax (Kan.) plant, which contains more than 1,100 robots. GM is now hiring back some laid-off workers to keep up with growing demand for stylish, high-quality new cars.

Or talk to Drew Greenblatt, president of Marlin Steel Wire Products in Baltimore [Md.], who pays his workers $30 an hour plus benefits and beats overseas companies that pay much less, thanks in part to investments in robotics technology. In the 12 years he's owned the wire basket and hook maker, Greenblatt has doubled head count while increasing revenue sixfold. Marlin exports products all over the world, including to Belgium, Poland, Switzerland, Australia, and Taiwan, as a result of the high-quality products his company produces.

Automation Is Good for America

The first industrial robot worldwide was installed in 1961 at a General Motors plant in New Jersey. Of the more than 1 million robots that work in manufacturing facilities worldwide, only a fifth are in U.S. factories. The relatively low adoption rate of robots in the U.S. is a hopeful sign, since we still have a chance to take advantage of robotics on a broader scale.

Industrial robotics also creates jobs at the companies that build and service the machines. Even though most of today's industrial robots are built in Japan and Europe, major robotics companies including ABB, Fanuc, Kuka Robotics, and Yaskawa Electric have U.S. divisions. Adept Technology is based in Pleasanton, Calif.

If you count robots working outside factories in fields including medicine, defense, and home maintenance, there are more than 8 million of the machines worldwide. Many leaders in those areas, including Intuitive Surgical Systems and iRobot, are based in the U.S.

Robot-building competitions like First Robotics, founded by inventor Dean Kamen, excite today's students who will become tomorrow's engineers and entrepreneurs.

There was a saying popular at General Electric in the '80s that American industry needed to "automate, emigrate, or evaporate". In the ensuing decades, we've lost too many jobs to emigration and evaporation. I hope more companies will choose to automate before it's too late.

Viewpoint 

> *"When increases in the minimum wage cause employers to eliminate entry-level jobs, potential employees are denied the opportunity to gain work skills and lose the ability to move up the economic ladder."*

Raising Minimum Wage Increases Unemployment

Christopher Jaarda

In the following viewpoint, Christopher Jaarda claims recent raises in minimum wage have helped foment the recession that began in 2007. Relying on historical data that suggest a correlation between minimum wage hikes and periods of high unemployment, Jaarda maintains that the current crisis has been exacerbated because businesses cannot afford to hire more unskilled labor when the cost of that labor increases. Christopher Jaarda is an attorney with the John Hancock Committee for the States, a conservative citizens organization. His previous experience includes working as a legal counsel and policy analyst for the Republican Policy Committee.

As you read, consider the following questions:

1. According to a poll by Greg Mankiw cited in Jaarda's viewpoint, what percentage of economists subscribe to the belief that raising minimum wage leads to higher unemployment for young unskilled workers?
2. Since 1990, how many times has Congress mandated a raise in the minimum wage, as reported by Jaarda?
3. According to the Bureau of Labor Statistics, how many people who did not finish high school or who graduated but did not go on to college have lost their jobs since July 2007?

Since the beginning of the current recession [December 2007], Democrats in Washington have blamed the economic downturn on "Wall Street greed," "predatory lending," "excessive deregulation," and "unrestrained capitalism." Rep. Barney Frank (D-MA) has even gone so far to say that "the private market got us into this mess, the government will have to get us out." Blaming capitalism for the recession may be useful for creating a political narrative, and for pushing progressive policies, but it ignores the real causes of the downturn. If Congress ignores or refuses to acknowledge these causes, there is a real danger that Congress will enact laws that could inhibit economic recovery (e.g., the stimulus, health care reform, cap and trade).

Some commentators have made the case that the recession can be traced to housing policies put in place by previous Congresses (policies like the Community Reinvestment Act and those that encouraged [mortgage finance companies] Fannie Mae and Freddie Mac to buy risky mortgages). Overlooked, perhaps, is the role that the current Democratic Congress may have played in creating the recession. While Speaker of the House Nancy Pelosi, Senate Majority Leader Harry Reid, and other Congressional Democrats have regularly claimed the bills they are trying to pass "will create jobs," their record on job creation belies such claims. The bill they passed in 2007 to increase the minimum wage increase is a perfect example.

Rising Unemployment Following Minimum Wage Hikes

Last year, Harvard University professor Greg Mankiw wrote that according to "various polls of the profession" 79% of economists subscribe to the following: "a minimum wage increases unemployment among young and unskilled workers." Generally speaking, economists believe that a minimum wage leads to higher unemployment for "unskilled" workers. It would also seem that there would be a correlation between an increase in the minimum wage and an increase in the national unemployment rate, particularly with respect to unskilled workers. It is worth examining the interchange of wage policies with unemployment.

In 2006, the Democrats campaigned on a promise to increase the minimum wage as part of their "Six for '06" agenda. In 2007, the new Democratic majority pushed through a $2.10 (or nearly 41%) increase in the minimum wage, phased in over three years beginning on July 24, 2007. When Congress passed this increase, the nation's unemployment rate was relatively low at 4.4%. Since then, it has increased steadily, peaking at 10.1% last October [2009].

While some might suggest any correlation between the increase in the minimum wage and the increase in unemployment is merely coincidental, historical data suggest there is a relationship between the two. Since 1970, Congress has enacted five minimum wage increases. According to the Bureau of Labor Statistics (BLS) data, unemployment rose dramatically immediately after four of those increases. The [accompanying] chart shows the relationship between unemployment and minimum wage increases over the past 40 years.

In 1974, Congress enacted a minimum wage increase (phased in over three years, 1974–1976). The month prior to the increase unemployment was 5.1%. Thereafter, unemployment immediately began to rise, peaking at 9.0% just 13 months later.

In 1978, Congress increased the minimum wage again (phased in over four years, 1978–1981). At the time of the first increase, unemployment was 6.4%. When the final increase was implemented, in 1981, unemployment was 7.5% and it increased to 10.8% by the end of the next year.

In 1990, Congress enacted another minimum wage increase. The month before the increase took effect, unemployment was 5.2%. With the increase, unemployment began to steadily increase and unemployment eventually peaked at 7.8%.

In 1996, when unemployment was 5.2%, Congress enacted another minimum wage increase. Unemployment rose slightly (to 5.4%) the next month but then declined slightly. This is the only instance in the last 40 years in which a federal minimum wage increase was not followed by an increase in unemployment.

Finally, in 2007, Congress enacted the latest increase (phased in over three years, 2007–2009). After each of the three incremental increases (in 2007, 2008 and 2009), unemployment has increased. The first wage increase took effect on July 24, 2007, when unemployment was 4.6%. A month later unemployment began moving upward and was up a half a point within 6 months. The next increase took effect in July 2008 when unemployment was 5.8%; six months later unemployment was 8.2%. In July 2009, when the final step of the wage increase kicked in, unemployment was 9.4% and it ticked upwards in each of the following three months (peaking at 10.1% by October). Accordingly, there seems to be a strong correlation between increases in the minimum wage and unemployment.

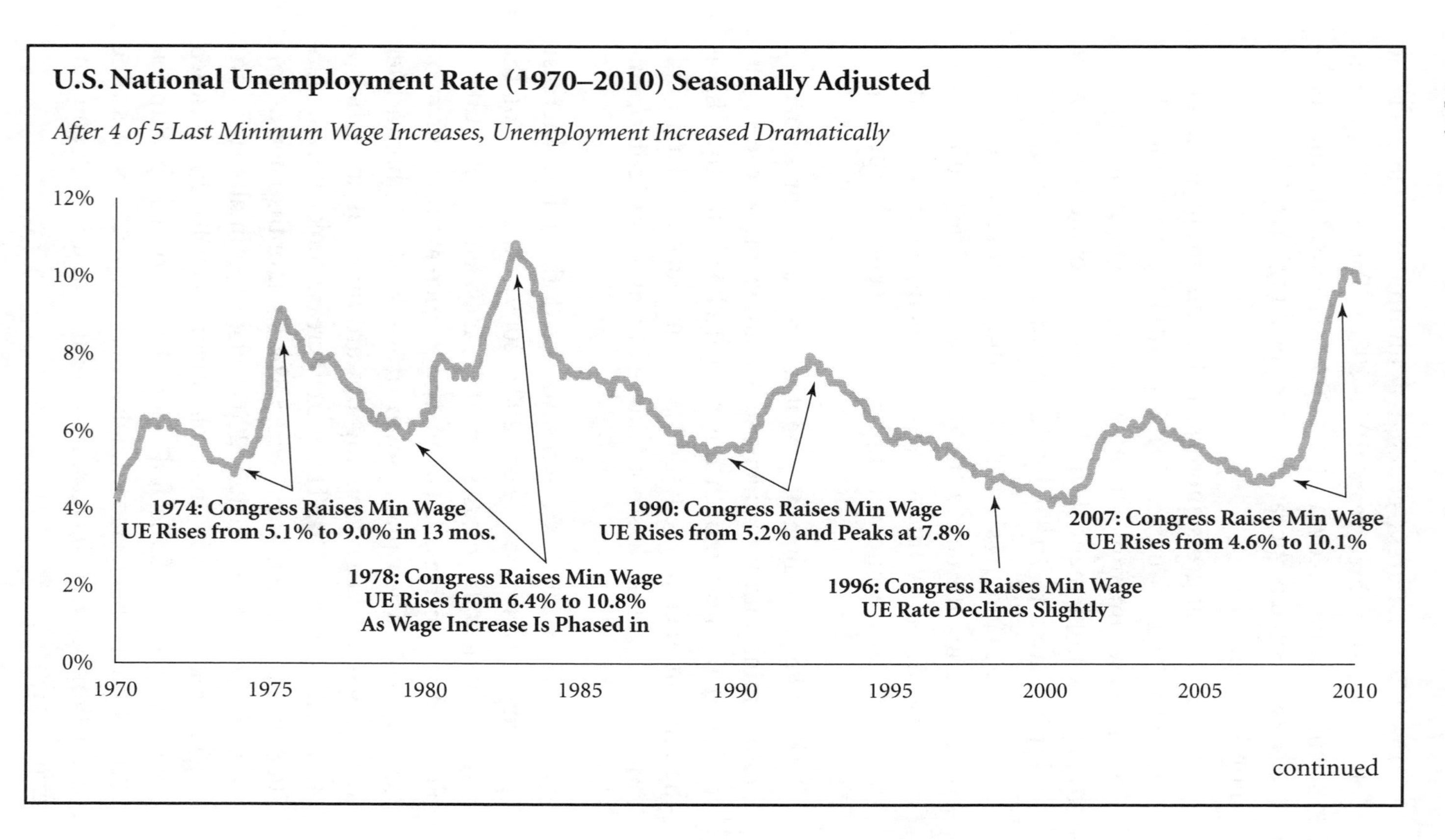
U.S. National Unemployment Rate (1970–2010) Seasonally Adjusted
After 4 of 5 Last Minimum Wage Increases, Unemployment Increased Dramatically
12%
10%
8%
6%
4%
2%
0%
1970
1975
1980
1985
1990
1995
2000
2005
2010
1974: Congress Raises Min Wage
UE Rises from 5.1% to 9.0% in 13 mos.
1978: Congress Raises Min Wage
UE Rises from 6.4% to 10.8%
As Wage Increase Is Phased in
1990: Congress Raises Min Wage
UE Rises from 5.2% and Peaks at 7.8%
1996: Congress Raises Min Wage
UE Rate Declines Slightly
2007: Congress Raises Min Wage
UE Rises from 4.6% to 10.1%

continued

U.S. Unemployment Rate by Education Level (1992–2010) [CONTINUED]

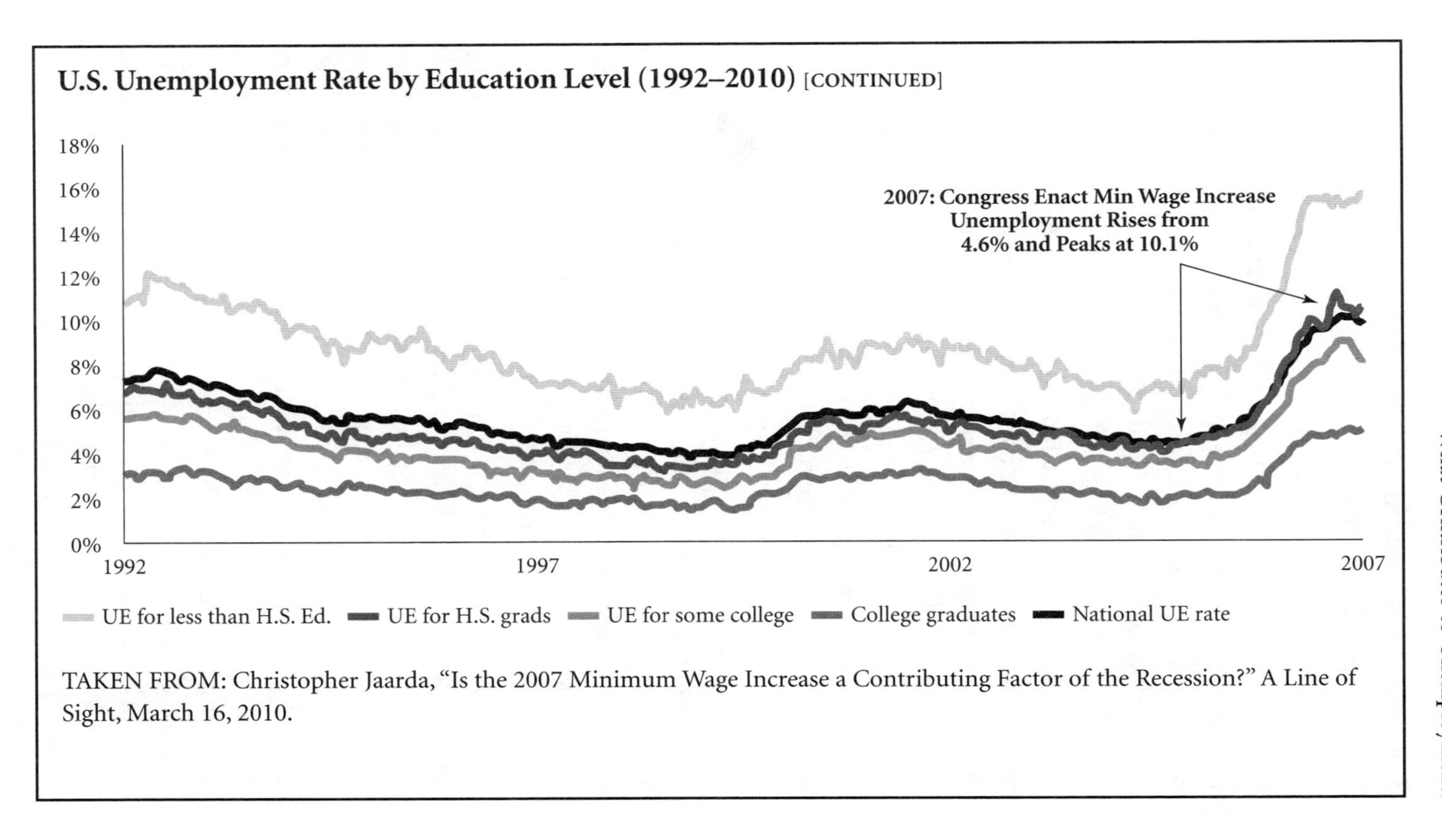

TAKEN FROM: Christopher Jaarda, "Is the 2007 Minimum Wage Increase a Contributing Factor of the Recession?" A Line of Sight, March 16, 2010.

Businesses Cannot Afford to Hire Costly Unskilled Labor

Consistent with the views of the economists cited by Professor Mankiw, the data show "unskilled" workers are harmed by minimum wage laws. During the current recession, unemployment has risen the most for people with less than a high school education (from 7.2% to 15.6% from July 2007 to February 2010 respectively).

The increase for high school dropouts is far greater than for people who are high school grads (rising from 4.5% to 10.5%), for those with some college (3.6% to 8.0%), or for those with a college degree (2.1% to 5.0%) during that time. In real terms, according to BLS, nearly 3.3 million people who did not complete high school or who graduated but did not go to college have lost their jobs since July 2007.

What accounts for this disparity? As Donald Boudreaux, a former economics professor, suggested in 2006: employers directly respond to higher labor costs. Boudreaux wrote: "[w]e don't know exactly how, or exactly by how much, employers as a group respond to higher minimum wages—but the theoretical case that they do respond in ways unfavorable to low-skilled employees is too powerful to dismiss."

The unfortunate thing is that these policies may have long-lasting effects on low-skilled workers. An entry-level job that pay's minimum wage is not just about wages. It is also about the skill and experience that an employee will gain. For those who are not seeking further education, this job, and the experience that comes with it, are critical to gaining the skills necessary to move up to a higher paying job. But when increases in the minimum wage cause employers to eliminate entry-level jobs, potential employees are denied the opportunity to gain work skills and lose the ability to move up the economic ladder. While they will eventually gain experience, the reality is that the lost employment opportunities brought on by

Congress' minimum wage policies may put these workers years behind in their ability to move up the economic ladder.

The paradox of past minimum wage increases is that while these increases were often championed by politicians claiming a desire to help "unskilled" or "low-skilled" American workers, these policies have had the perverse effect of increasing unemployment among the very individuals they were intended to help. Therefore, the Democratic Congress' economic policies have actually made it harder for unskilled workers to find employment and have destroyed, rather than created, opportunity and upward economic mobility.

VIEWPOINT 6

"Extensive research refutes the claim that increasing the minimum wage causes increased unemployment and business closures."

Raising Minimum Wage Does Not Increase Unemployment

Holly Sklar

In the following viewpoint—a broadsheet from the Let Justice Roll Campaign—Holly Sklar claims that raising the minimum wage will not increase unemployment. Instead, she argues that raising the minimum wage will speed recovery from economic recessions by giving more spending money to lower-income families. Sklar is an author and syndicated columnist, policy analyst, and strategist whose articles have appeared in hundreds of newspapers and online outlets. She is the director of the Let Justice Roll Living Wage Campaign, an organization that seeks to raise the minimum wage.

As you read, consider the following questions:

1. Instead of rising wages, what does Sklar say is currently fueling America's economy?

Holly Sklar, "Raising the Minimum Wage in Hard Times," Let Justice Roll Living Wage Campaign, July 22, 2009.

2. When did the buying power of the minimum wage peak, according to Sklar?
3. As the author reports, what was the longest period in U.S. history that did not witness a minimum wage increase?

The federal minimum wage was not enacted during good times, but during the extraordinarily hard times of the Great Depression. When the federal minimum wage was established in 1938, the unemployment rate was still a very high 19 percent.

President Franklin Roosevelt called the minimum wage "an essential part of economic recovery." It would put a floor under worker wages, alleviate the hardship of inadequate wages, and stimulate the economy and job creation by increasing consumer purchasing power. The federal minimum wage was also meant to promote economic development and stop the original "race to the bottom" of employers moving to cheaper labor states in a downward spiral.

In his January 3, 1938 annual message to Congress, calling for passage of the historic Fair Labor Standards Act, Roosevelt said, millions of workers "receive pay so low that they have little buying power. Aside from the undoubted fact that they thereby suffer great human hardship, they are unable to buy adequate food and shelter, to maintain health or to buy their share of manufactured goods."

Roosevelt said, "The increase of national purchasing power [is] an underlying necessity of the day." And so it is today.

Many Workers Lack the Money to Pay for Necessities

Consumer spending makes up about 70% of our economy. The minimum wage sets the wage floor. A low minimum wage institutionalizes an increasingly low-wage workforce.

Even after the increase to $7.25, the minimum wage will be lower than the $7.93 minimum wage of 1956 and much lower than 1968's $9.92, adjusting for inflation.

A growing share of workers make too little to buy necessities—much less afford a middle-class standard of living. More and more two-paycheck households struggle to afford a home, college, healthcare and retirement once normal for middle-class households with one paycheck.

There has been a massive shift of income from the bottom and middle to the top. By 2006, the richest 1% of Americans had increased their share of the nation's income to the second-highest level on record. The only year higher was 1928—on the eve of the Great Depression.

- In 1973, the richest 1% of Americans had 9% of national income. By 2006, they had 23%.

As we are seeing so painfully, an economy fueled by rising debt, greed and speculation, rather than rising wages, is a house of cards.

"When businesses don't pay a living wage all society pays," said U.S. Women's Chamber of Commerce CEO Margot Dorfman in signing a statement by national business leaders and small business owners from every state supporting a minimum wage increase. "We pay through poverty and needless disease, disability and death from inadequate healthcare. We pay as women struggle to put food on the table. We pay as businesses and communities suffer economic decline."

America's Economy Is Not Working for American Workers

Let Justice Roll predicted the economic meltdown in our first report, *A Just Minimum Wage: Good for Workers, Business and Our Future*, in 2005. We called for an end to the low-wage, low-social responsibility low road, saying, "The high road is not only the better road, it is the only road for progress in the future. An America that doesn't work for working people is not an America that works. We will not prosper economically or ethically in the global economy relying on low wages, outsourcing and debt in place of innovation and opportunity. We will not prosper in the global economy relying on disinvestment in place of reinvestment. We can't succeed that way any more than farmers can 'compete' by eating their seed corn."

We said, "The United States is an increasingly shaky superpower with a hollowed-out manufacturing base, large trade deficit and growing debt held heavily by other countries. Households have propped themselves up in the face of falling real wages by maxing out work hours, credit cards and home equity loans . . . This is not a sustainable course . . . The low road is like a 'shortcut' that leads to a cliff."

We have fallen off the cliff.

Underpaid workers and responsible businesses are bailing out banks and corporations run by reckless overpaid bosses who milked their companies and our country like cash cows—and trashed the global economy. Enough is enough.

Boosting Consumer Purchasing Power and Economic Recovery

We hear a lot of talk about the importance of consumer spending to recovery from our current economic crisis. Well, consumers can't spend what they don't have.

If consumer purchasing power is at the heart of economic recovery, wages are at the heart of consumer purchasing power.

Minimum wage workers, like all workers, are also consumers. Minimum wage raises are well-targeted stimulus because they go directly to those who most need to spend additional dollars on food, fuel, housing, healthcare and other necessities.

Minimum wage workers don't put raises into Wall Street's many Ponzi schemes [i.e., investment scams], commodity speculation or offshore tax havens. They recycle their raises back into local businesses and the economy by buying needed goods and services.

According to the Economic Policy Institute report, *A Stealthy Stimulus: How boosting the minimum wage is helping to stimulate the economy*, the first two minimum wage increases "will have generated an estimated $4.9 billion of spending by July 2009, precisely when our economy needed it the most. The final increase in July 2009 is expected to generate another $5.5 billion over the following year."

Raising the Minimum Wage Does Not Increase Unemployment

Critics routinely oppose minimum wage increases in good times and bad, claiming they will increase unemployment, no matter the real world record to the contrary. Extensive research refutes the claim that increasing the minimum wage causes increased unemployment and business closures....

The buying power of the minimum wage reached its peak in 1968. The unemployment rate went from 3.8% in 1967 to 3.6% in 1968 to 3.5% in 1969. The next time the unemployment rate came close to those levels was after the minimum wage raises of 1996 and 1997.

As *BusinessWeek* put it in 2001, "Many economists have backed away from the argument that minimum wage [laws] lead to fewer jobs."

The decade between the federal minimum wage increase to $5.15 an hour on Sept. 1, 1997 and the July 24, 2007 increase to $5.85 was the longest period in history without a raise. Numerous states raised their minimum wages higher than the federal level during that period. Research by the Fiscal Policy Institute and others showed that states that raised their minimum wages above the federal level experienced better employment and small business trends than states that did not.

Three important newer studies, carefully controlling for non-minimum wage variables, published by the Institute for Research on Labor and Employment (Univ. of Calif., Berkeley), further advanced the research on minimum wage employment effects. *Minimum Wage Effects Across State Borders* compared all neighboring counties in the U.S. located on different sides of a state border with different minimum wage levels between 1990 and 2006 and found no adverse employment effects from higher minimum wages.

Do Minimum Wages Really Reduce Teen Employment? analyzed the 1990–2007 period, which includes the last two recessions (July 1990 to March 1991 and March 2001 to November 2001) as well as the 2007 minimum wage increase. Researchers found no significant teen employment loss due to minimum wage increases. *Spacial Heterogeneity and Minimum Wages: Employment Estimates for Teens Using Cross-State Commuting Zones* furthers the research, finding "no discernable disemployment effect, even when minimum wage increases lead to relatively large wage changes."

Raise the Floor to Lift the Economy

The minimum wage sets the wage floor. As Roosevelt and his advisers understood, we have to raise the floor to lift the economy.

Frances Perkins was Secretary of Labor from 1933 to 1945 and the first woman to serve in a presidential cabinet. She accepted the position after securing Roosevelt's commitment to champion the minimum wage, a 40-hour workweek, unemployment insurance, Social Security and other hallmarks of the New Deal. In 1933, while still serving as Industrial Commissioner of the New York State Department of Labor, Perkins wrote in the magazine, *Survey Graphic*, about the real "cost of a five-dollar dress":

> It hangs in the window of one of the little cash-and-carry stores that now line a street where fashionable New Yorkers

> used to drive out in their carriages to shop at Tiffany's and Constable's. It is a "supper dress" of silk crepe in "the new red" . . . A cardboard tag on the shoulder reads: "Special $4.95." Bargain basements and little ready-to-wear shops are filled with similar "specials."
>
> But the manufacturer who pays a living wage for a reasonable week's work under decent conditions cannot turn out attractive silk frocks to retail at $5 or less . . .
>
> If the purchaser does not pay a price that allows for a subsistence wage and reasonable hours and working conditions, then the cost of the "bargain" must be sweated out of the workers.
>
> The red silk bargain dress in the shop window is a danger signal. It is a warning of the return of the sweatshop, a challenge to us all to reinforce the gains we have made in our long and difficult progress towards a civilized industrial order.

Perkins wanted the minimum wage to be a living wage. The Department of Labor is located in the Frances Perkins Building. It's time to stop undoing Perkins' legacy and build on it.

Paying workers enough to live on should not be optional—in good times or bad.

Periodical Bibliography

The following articles have been selected to supplement the diverse views presented in this chapter.

Economist	"Extension Deficit Disorder," June 12, 2010.
Rana Foroohar	"Joblessness Is Here to Stay," *Newsweek*, December 21, 2009.
Barry C. Lynn and Phillip Longman	"Who Broke America's Jobs Machine?" *Washington Monthly*, March/April 2010.
George Mannes	"How You'll Know Employment Is on the Upswing," *Money*, April 2010.
Paul Craig Roberts	"The Rich Have Stolen the Economy," *Catholic New Times*, November 16, 2009.
Robert J. Samuelson	"The Reluctant Recovery," *Newsweek*, June 21, 2010.
William F. Shughart II	"Unemployment Then and Now," *Independent*, Spring 2010.
Eve Tahmincioglu	"Working for Free," *Time*, April 12, 2010.
David Von Drehle	"Yes, We Still Make Stuff," *Time*, May 25, 2009.
Wall Street Journal	"Mandating Unemployment," July 14, 2009.
James Warren	"The Mystery of Welfare and the Recession," *Bloomberg BusinessWeek*, May 24, 2010.

Chapter 2

Who Is Particularly Affected by High Unemployment?

Chapter Preface

Unemployment rates do not affect all segments of the population evenly. For many years, observers have warned that outsourcing and other structural changes in American manufacturing industries have put many unskilled laborers into welfare lines. In the wake of the most recent financial crisis, the unemployment of unskilled workers has risen even more. In May 2010, the Bureau of Labor Statistics (BLS) reported that the U.S. unemployment rate for people without a high school diploma was 15 percent, while those with at least a bachelor's degree registered only 4.7 percent unemployment. "Increasingly, employees need minds, not just bodies," John Silvia, chief economist for Wells Fargo, told the *Philadelphia Inquirer*. "This has been a major source of economic as well as political unrest as, increasingly, many workers realize their skills do not meet the needs of the workplace."

Although some analysts like Silvia recognize the economy is shedding many unskilled positions, other experts point out that several factors influence the unemployment rate of unskilled workers. In testimony before the House Judiciary Subcommittee on Immigration on November 19, 2009, Steven A. Camarota of the Center for Immigration Studies argued that massive immigration in recent years has led to greater competition among unskilled native and immigrant laborers. "Almost all economists agree that less-educated workers have done very poorly in the labor market over the past four decades as immigration has increased," Camarota's argument begins. He explains that new immigrants tend to work for the lowest wages and often find positions within their communities where employers of the same ethnic background are disposed to hire them. Such preferences tend to reduce the demand for native unskilled workers—especially black workers and high school youths.

Another factor that some analysts point to is the increase in the minimum wage. Economics professor Mark J. Perry wrote an online article for the *Wall Street Journal* on March 6, 2010, that used BLS statistics to chart the last three increases in the minimum wage versus the unemployment rate of unskilled teenagers. Perry found that since 2002, "each of the three minimum wage increases was accompanied by about a 2 percentage point increase in the amount that the teenage jobless rate exceeded the overall rate." Others have blamed such increases on the loss of jobs for other sectors of the unskilled labor pool. On June 15, 2010, Sara Williams, a guest blogger on the Adam Smith Institute Blog, asserted that the reasoning behind the negative impact of wage increases is straightforward. "The lowest paid unskilled workers are let go because the value of the work is lower than the price," She writes. Instead of paying the high price for unskilled labor, Williams states "the employer will increase hours of higher skilled workers already employed or decrease production."

In the following chapter, various employment analysts examine the impact of the current recession on different segments of the population. These various experts claim that minorities, as well as the young and the old, are more severely affected by fiscal downturns than the general population.

Viewpoint 

"A large segment of the black population has simply been hit harder than everyone else."

Black Unemployment Is Higher than the National Average

Joel Dreyfuss

In the following viewpoint, Joel Dreyfuss reports that while America's jobless rate has finally declined below 10 percent in the recent recession, black unemployment is nearly twice the national average. Dreyfuss points out that plenty of African Americans are gainfully employed, but the prevalence of blacks in urban centers where major industries have shut down—such as in Gary, Indiana, and Flint, Michigan—has left many trapped in poverty and joblessness. Dreyfuss worries that these blighted communities will be forgotten as the country embraces "pulling oneself up by one's bootstraps" policies during the hard economic times. Joel Dreyfuss is the managing editor of TheRoot.com, a webzine that focuses on issues relevant to the black community. He previously served in editorial positions at Fortune, PC Magazine, *and* Black Enterprise.

Joel Dreyfuss, "Black Unemployment Is Not News," *The Root*, February 7, 2010.

As you read, consider the following questions:

1. According to recent polls reported by Dreyfuss, what percentage of African American men are unemployed?
2. According to Dreyfuss, what sector of the economy employs a lot of blacks and often shrinks during periods of recession?
3. Why does William Julius Wilson claim that President Barack Obama will not likely make a special effort to immediately help blacks during the economic crisis?

Why 16.5 percent joblessness among African-Americans hardly rates a mention. Despair has become banal.

It's interesting how some numbers don't make the news. Friday's [February 5, 2010] announcement that unemployment in the U.S. had dropped to 9.5 percent was welcome, even if the gains turn out fragile or illusory. Most of the early news stories left out an even bigger number: black unemployment at 16.5 percent, black male unemployment a whopping 17.6 percent. Since the rules of journalism require that the most important information come first, the overall national figures deserve first billing. In a lot of newsrooms, the crisis of joblessness among black Americans is no longer news. It drops to the bottom, or, when time and space run out, out of the story completely.

Routine News Stories of Black America

The banality of despair is part of the American tradition. Having nearly one of five men unemployed in certain communities is devastating but hardly newsworthy when recession is a permanent state. Poverty is nothing new in America. At one point or the other, various groups have endured the role of being at the bottom of the economic ladder: the Chinese, the Germans, the Irish, the Italians, the Jews. Each wave has played through the pain, to borrow a phrase from sports. And for the most part, each group of newcomers has, over time, advanced to the better life that America offered.

African-Americans are undoubtedly a special case; most have been here longer than everyone but the Native Americans and the Mayflower blue-bloods (who, incidentally, created full employment by importing slaves from Africa). In the 45 years since black Americans won "full" citizenship through the Civil Rights Acts, a significant number have benefitted from their new rights. Behaving very much like recent immigrants, they have climbed the social ladder. They have prospered, become educated, moved to better neighborhoods and sent their children to good schools. African-Americans have made significant advances in American society. They have become CEOs, heads of federal departments, mayors and Congressmen, senior officials in foundations, school principals, bankers, journalists, entertainers, professional athletes, academics, civil servants and small business owners. And there's even President [Barack] Obama.

The routine of black life in American has plenty of successes today, a significant change from just 50 years ago, when black Americans could not eat, sleep, live and work in large parts of America. Just recently we [*The Root*] ran a story about a black investment group that rescued the Iridium satellite phone company from extinction and sold it at a healthy profit. The CEO of Xerox is a black woman and that is almost routine, now that there have been a half-dozen black CEOs of Fortune 500 companies. Neither has been found terribly newsworthy either. These stories have become routine, too.

Joblessness and Suffering

But a large segment of the black population has simply been hit harder than everyone else. That's indisputable fact. There are a number of reasons. Many of the cities where black Americans are concentrated are in the Rust Belt [manufacturing regions]; St. Louis [Mo.], Detroit [Mich.], Cleveland

Presidential Inaction

Despite [a] historic level of support in the election, [President Barack] Obama continues to treat African Americans as political strangers, if not a political afterthought. Black male unemployment is the highest it has been since the Second World War, Black poverty is on the rise, African Americans are losing their homes at breakneck speed—and meanwhile, the first African American president fiddles while Rome—or in this case, Harlem [N.Y.], Englewood [Ill.], Lawndale [Ill.] and Detroit [Mich.], among others—burns. . . .

During the campaign, he promised to do even less for African Americans, fearing to be painted as "the Black president"—the result is that he is now going out of his way to ignore the particular problems in African American communities resulting from the disproportionate impact of the economic crisis.

Keenanga-Yamatta Taylor, "Black America's Economic Freefall," SocialistWorker.org, January 8, 2010. http://socialistworker.org.

[Ohio], Buffalo [N.Y.], Baltimore [Md.]. The jobs in the steel mills of Gary, Indiana and the auto plants of Flint, Michigan that made possible the American Dream for millions of blacks and whites in the 1950s and 60s are gone. They went South to union-free plants and to Brazil, or east to Indonesia, China and other places where wages are in the single digits per hour. African-Americans are also concentrated in service jobs, a vulnerable sector that shrinks rapidly in recession.

The latest U.S. Census estimates report that black median family income was just over $41,000 in 2008, the lowest in the U.S. of any racial group. A single black woman with children earned a median annual income of $25,958 in 2008, according to the Census estimates. No surprise then, that one out of five black families lives in poverty. More than 40 percent of black families headed by a single mom are poor.

Does the U.S. government have an obligation to create special programs to address the severe afflictions in the African-American community? This essentially political question has been the same for about a half century. But it acquires new tension in the age of Obama. What makes the answer more complicated is the fact that the President of the United States is black. Barack Obama may have transcended race in achieving the White House, but he also knows that transcendence is fragile and quickly exhausted and that a certain segment of Americans look for signs that he favors one group of Americans (blacks) over another.

Washington Post columnist Courtland Milloy raised the issue of making a special effort last fall with Harvard sociologist William Julius Wilson, an expert on black unemployment. "Obama can't just talk about blacks when all groups are experiencing incredible jobless rates and suffering," Wilson told Milloy. "I believe he'll get around to addressing racial disparities in the long term, but in the short term he's got to talk about a stimulus package that increases unemployment benefits and reduces joblessness across the board."

Milloy wrote: "Still, as Wilson knows well, black people are affected far more adversely by these soaring rates of unemployment. So does Obama. So do all Americans. With midterm elections looming, the President has begun to talk about creating jobs. He knows that he will be punished by the electorate for high unemployment, even if it's not his fault nor as bad as it would have been without his stimulus bill."

The Bootstraps Model Returns

But the willingness to focus on the most blighted segment of America is directly proportional to how much Americans really believe that black Americans are somehow to blame for their own high unemployment. After all, in the new "post-racial" era nary a word is heard about affirmative action or reparations. We're back to an ahistorical narrative of America; everyone has bootstraps; it's up to you to pull yourself up. Government plays no role, or at best a minimal one.

So far, all indications are that the President will continue to focus on the "big picture." That will get him re-elected. Addressing black unemployment is a lose-lose when even the most dire conditions don't even make the headlines. So numbers like 16.5 percent and 17.6 percent will stay at the bottom of the news story, and, all too often, get crowded out completely by more important events.

VIEWPOINT 2

> *"The Great Recession derailed the gains that Hispanics had achieved relative to the overall labor force."*

Hispanic Unemployment Is Higher than the National Average

U.S. Congress' Joint Economic Committee

The following viewpoint is an excerpt from a congressional report on unemployment among the Hispanic community in America. In the viewpoint, the Joint Economic Committee asserts that the jobless rate for Hispanics exceeds the national average. The committee blames this fact on the shrinking construction sector (where many Hispanics are typically employed) and the lack of Hispanics represented in higher-paying growth industries such as education and health care. The committee also emphasizes that many Hispanics in America are working fewer hours than other workers because they are stuck in part-time jobs instead of full-time positions. Congress' Joint Economic Committee is chaired by New York Representative Carolyn B. Maloney.

As you read, consider the following questions:

1. According to the Joint Economic Committee, what was the jobless rate for Hispanic men in March 2010?
2. As the committee explains, what two sectors of the unemployed does the U-6 measure take into account that more traditional measures of unemployment do not?
3. What economic factor does the committee blame for the significant rise in Hispanic unemployment during the current recession?

Since the Bureau of Labor Statistics began tracking unemployment rates by race and ethnicity, the unemployment rate for Hispanic workers has been consistently higher than the overall unemployment rate. Despite the relative difficulties faced by Hispanic workers, there was reason to be optimistic in May 2006, as the gap between the Hispanic unemployment rate (4.9 percent) and the overall unemployment rate (4.6 percent) reached a record low of 0.3 percentage points. Coinciding with the steady progress made by Hispanic workers—many of whom were employed in the construction industry—was the boom in the housing market, with home prices peaking in mid-2006. However, when home prices started plummeting from their peak and the housing market began its collapse, the gains made by Hispanics evaporated. By October 2009—three and half years after the disparity between the unemployment rates of Hispanics and the rest of the population reached its low point—the Hispanic unemployment rate climbed to 13.1 percent, 3 percentage points higher than the overall unemployment rate of 10.1 percent. While the disparity has dropped slightly in the last few months [Spring 2010], the Hispanic unemployment rate in March 2010 was 12.6 percent, 2.9 percentage points higher than the overall unemployment rate of 9.7 percent. In absolute terms, out of the 22.7

million Hispanics that comprised the U.S. labor force (14.8 percent of the total) in March, 2.9 million were unemployed (19.1 percent of the total).

The Great Recession [the longest economic downturn in the United States of the post-World War II era, officially lasting from December 2007 to June 2009] derailed the gains that Hispanics had achieved relative to the overall labor force. Since the housing bubble may have contributed much to the progress made by Hispanic workers, a long process of sectoral reallocation within the Hispanic labor force may be part of what is necessary for them to once again approach parity with the overall labor force.

Hispanic Jobless Rates on the Rise

As job losses mounted during the recession, unemployment among Hispanic men rose to troubling levels. The disparity between this rate and the overall unemployment rate of men also grew. While the unemployment rate for all men rose by 6.8 percentage points to 11.8 percent between March 2007 and March 2010, the jobless rate for Hispanic men climbed by 8.2 percentage points, reaching 13.8 percent in March 2010.

Hispanic women also experienced jobless rates higher than those for all women prior to the start of the current recession. In March 2007, the unemployment rate among Hispanic women was 5.1 percent, compared to 4.1 percent among all women, Most recently, the jobless rate for Latinas, 12.5 percent in March 2010, was 4.2 percentage points higher than the unemployment rate for all women.

The weak labor market has hit Hispanic workers of all age groups more heavily than it has hit the overall labor force. In March 2010, nearly one-third—30.1 percent—of Hispanic teens (those between ages 16 to 19) were unemployed, compared with one-quarter (25.3 percent) of all teens. A similar pattern emerges when comparing Hispanic and overall unemployment rates across various age groups. Among younger

Hispanic workers (those between ages 20 and 24), 18.2 percent were unemployed, compared to the overall unemployment rate of younger workers, 15.8 percent. Prime-age Hispanic workers (those between the ages of 25 and 54) had an unemployment rate of 11.9 percent, 2.4 percentage points higher than the overall unemployment rate of prime-age workers. Hispanic workers over 55 but under 65 had an unemployment rate of 7.3 percent compared to the unemployment rate for all workers in that age category of 9.5 percent. The largest discrepancy is among older workers (those over 65). Older Hispanic workers had an unemployment rate of 12.3 percent, compared with an overall unemployment rate of older workers of 6.9 percent. The larger gap may be attributable to the fact that Hispanic workers are more likely to be employed in occupations requiring manual labor, and employers may be less likely to fill these positions with older workers. In addition, Hispanic workers have persistently earned 25 to 31 percent less than the median weekly earnings of all employees, and these workers may not have sufficient retirement savings, and may be more likely to remain in the labor force looking for employment. In the first quarter of 2010, median usual weekly earnings on Hispanic workers were $554, compared to $754 for all workers.

Why Jobs Remain Elusive

The current economic downturn has been characterized by exceptionally long spells of unemployment. As of March 2010, 42.8 percent of the 6.7 million unemployed Americans had been out of work for 27 weeks or more, and the typical unemployment spell lasted 21.6 weeks. While some demographic groups, such as African Americans, are experiencing disproportionate shares of long-term unemployment, Latinos actually experience less long-term unemployment as a share of the unemployed (38.1 percent) and shorter unemployment spells (18.9 weeks) than the overall labor force. Although the typical

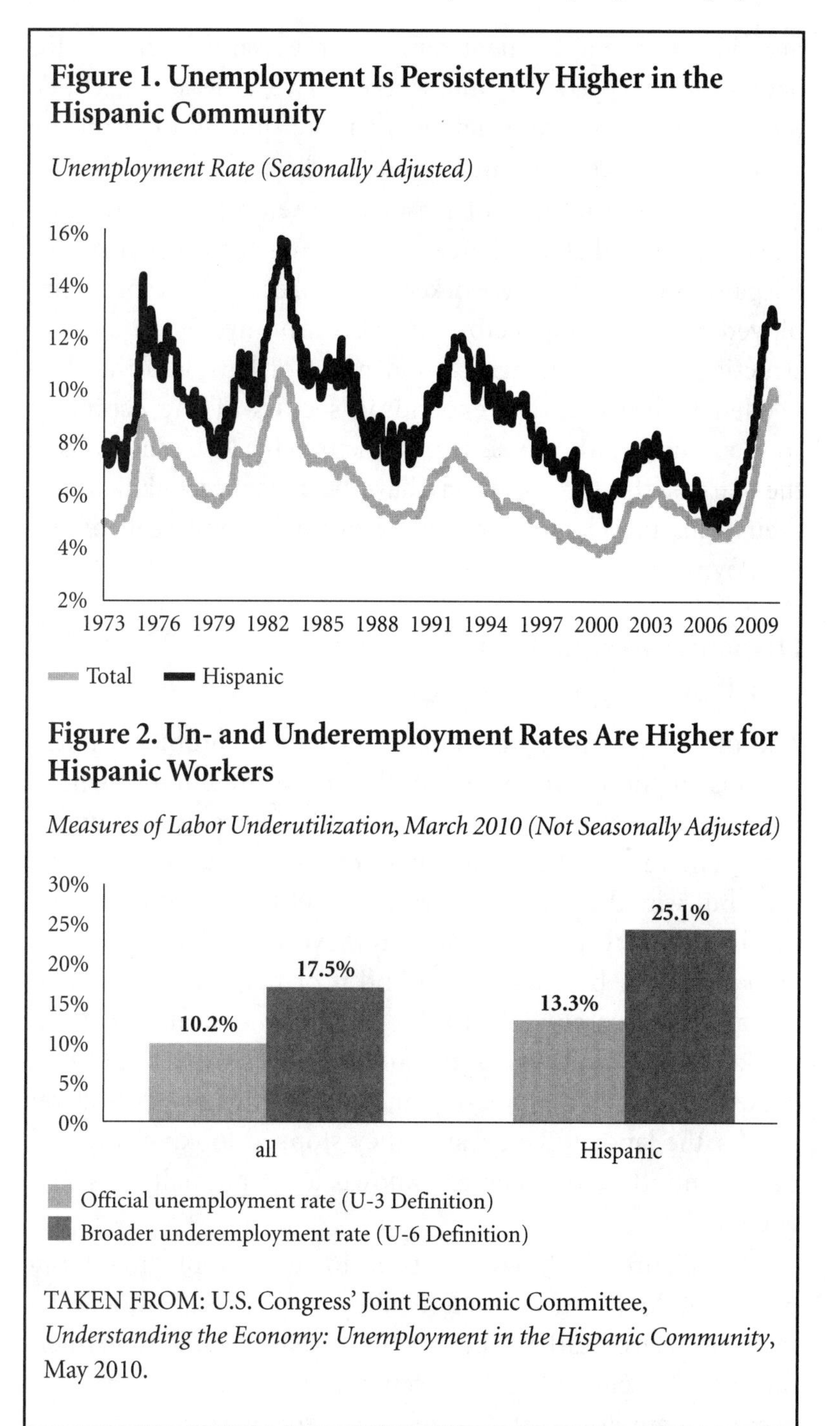

Figure 1. Unemployment Is Persistently Higher in the Hispanic Community

Figure 2. Un- and Underemployment Rates Are Higher for Hispanic Workers

TAKEN FROM: U.S. Congress' Joint Economic Committee, *Understanding the Economy: Unemployment in the Hispanic Community*, May 2010.

duration of unemployment remains at a record high for Hispanics, unemployed Hispanic workers have, at least to date, either managed to secure new work more quickly or drop out of the labor force more than other workers.

There are a number of reasons that employment remains elusive for a substantial number of long-term unemployed Hispanic workers. These workers were likely to have been employed in shrinking sectors of the economy—such as construction or manufacturing—and may not have had the skills needed to move to the expanding sectors of the economy, such as the healthcare sector. Workers who lost their jobs at the start of the recession may have been the least skilled, and their skills may have deteriorated during a long spell of unemployment.

Hispanic Marginal Employment and Underemployment

The official unemployment rate understates problems facing Latinos in the labor force. An alternative underemployment measure known as the "U-6" starts with the traditional unemployment rate and includes workers who are working part time but would prefer to be working full time. These workers, the involuntary part-timers, may have looked for full-time work and have been unable to find it or have had their hours cut at their current job. In addition, the U-6 also includes workers who would like a job, are available to work, and have looked for work in the last year, but they are not considered part of the labor force because they stopped looking for work over a month ago—they are known as "marginally attached workers."

As [Figure 2] shows, the traditional unemployment rate masks the high rate of underemployment in the Latino labor force. In March 2010, Latino workers had an unemployment rate of 13.3 percent, 3.1 percentage points higher than the overall unemployment rate of 10.2 percent (comparing seasonally unadjusted data). However, the U-6 or underemployment rate for Latino workers was 25.1 percent, 11.8 percentage points higher than the conventional unemployment rate. For the overall labor force, the U-6 rate was 17.5 percent, which is 7.3 percentage points higher than the conventional unemployment rate. The differences in the U-6 rate between Hispanics and the overall population can be attributed to the higher share of unemployed and involuntary part-time workers in the Hispanic community. However, when it comes to the portion of workers who are marginally attached to the labor force, there is no substantial difference between Hispanic workers and the overall population. The larger gap between the traditional unemployment rate and the broader U-6 rate among Hispanics suggests that while underemployment is inarguably a significant problem for the overall labor force, it is an even greater problem for the Hispanic community.

Collapsed Industries and Burst Housing Bubbles

Prior to the start of the recession, Hispanics were more likely to work in industries such as construction, manufacturing, and leisure and hospitality—all sectors that experienced large job losses during the Great Recession. But most of the increase in the unemployment rate in the Latino community appears to be caused by the bursting of the housing bubble. Employment in the construction sector reached a peak of 7.7 million workers in August 2006. By February 2010, however, employment had dropped by well over a quarter (27.8 percent) to 5.6 million workers. In 2007, roughly one-in-seven (14.7 percent) Latinos worked in the construction industry, compared with one-in-twelve (8.1 percent) workers in the overall labor force.

Similarly, Hispanic workers were more likely to be employed in leisure and hospitality jobs, a sector that contracted by 4 percent over the course of the recession. In 2007, 11.8

percent of the Hispanic workforce was employed in leisure and hospitality sector compared to 8.5 percent of the overall labor force.

While job losses in the manufacturing sector alone may explain some of the rise in the unemployment rate among Hispanic workers, losses in the manufacturing sector do not explain the difference in the rise in unemployment between Hispanic workers and the overall labor force. While employment in the manufacturing sector fell by 16 percent from December 2007 to December 2009, Hispanic workers were only slightly over-represented in this industry sector. At the start of the recession, 11.6 percent of the Hispanic workforce was employed in the manufacturing sector compared to 11.2 percent of the overall population.

Further exacerbating unemployment during the recession, Hispanics also were significantly less likely to work in education and health services, an industry that expanded 4 percent between December 2007 and December 2009, even in the wake of widespread job losses across other sectors. In 2007, only 14.4 percent of employed Latinos were working in the education and health services industry, compared with 21.0 percent of the overall employed population.

Geographic differences may also explain part of the sharp rise in the Hispanic unemployment rate during this recession. Many states with large concentrations of Hispanic workers, such as California, Florida, and Nevada, have faced large employment losses and corresponding increases in the unemployment rate. These also happened to be the states that suffered tremendously from the collapse of the housing market.

While home prices nationwide fell 30.8 percent from the peak in March 2006 to the trough in April 2009, home prices in Nevada, Arizona, Florida, and California fell by much more than the national average. Only two states with large Latino populations, Texas and New Mexico, saw smaller home price declines and lower foreclosure rates than the national average.

At the same time, Nevada, Arizona, Florida, and California saw large increases in foreclosure rates. In the first quarter of 2007, foreclosure rates in these states were under 1.2 percent, but then increased rapidly as the recession progressed. For example, by the end of 2009, the foreclosure rate was 9.8 percent in Nevada and 13.4 percent in Florida, while the national foreclosure rate was 4.6 percent. . . .

Needed Recovery Policies

Policies to create jobs during the recovery must ensure that the unemployment rate drops for all workers, regardless of race or ethnicity. Hispanic workers are over-represented in certain industries that either may not be expanding or may grow slowly during the recovery, and targeted policies to make sure that these workers have the skills to move into expanding sectors may be necessary. Additional policies to encourage mobility of the labor force from states still experiencing a housing slump may also be warranted. Members of the Hispanic community will undoubtedly benefit from job-creation and training policies that are designed to reduce unemployment, but policies that target specific sectors and regions may be more effective at combating Hispanic unemployment.

VIEWPOINT

"American Indians have had a lower employment-to-population ratio than whites over the entire recession."

Native American Unemployment Is Higher than the National Average

Algernon Austin

In the following viewpoint, Algernon Austin recounts that the "Great Recession"—the economic crisis that began with the 2007 banking failures—has led to widespread unemployment in the United States. As Austin relates, the crisis has had extremely negative effects on the Native American community, increasing unemployment among many tribes across the country. Austin contends that the Native Americans' unemployment levels exceed national averages in many regions and that Native Americans have disproportionate rates of unemployment when compared with whites in the same areas. Austin worries that these high rates are worsening already-existing disparities and will deepen Native American poverty. Algernon Austin is a sociologist of racial relations and the director of the Race, Ethnicity, and the Economy Program at the Economic Policy Institute.

As you read, consider the following questions:

1. As Austin reports, how many percentage points higher was the white employment rate than the Native American rate in the first half of 2009?
2. As Austin recounts, in what region of the United States was the decline in the Native American employment rate roughly equal to the decline in the employment rate for whites in the first half of 2009?
3. In what region of the United States has Native American unemployment nearly tripled over the recession, according to Austin?

American Indians, like Hispanic Americans and African Americans, have had the misfortune of experiencing double-digit unemployment rates for most or all of 2009. In the first half of this year, the American Indian unemployment rate averaged 13.6%. This rate is up from 7.8% in the last half of 2007, and it is 5.4 percentage points higher than the comparable 2009 white rate. All groups are being hurt by the Great Recession [the longest economic downturn in the U.S. of the post-World War II era, officially lasting from December 2007 to June 2009], but the pain is more severe in communities of color.

To be counted as unemployed, one has to be actively looking for work at the time of being surveyed. Individuals experiencing long spells of unemployment or who have an especially difficult time finding work are more likely to drop out of the labor force by not actively looking for work. The Great Recession has caused large numbers of workers to drop out of the labor force.

For some groups, however, even during non-recessionary times, they experience long spells of unemployment and a difficult time finding work. American Indians, African Americans, and teens are three such groups. For these groups, it is useful to examine the employment-to-population ratio or the employment rate. The employment rate simply identifies what portion of the working-age population is working. All individuals without jobs are counted as not working whether or not they are actively looking for work at the time of the survey.

Greater Unemployment for Native Americans

American Indians have had a lower employment-to-population ratio than whites over the entire recession. In the latter half of 2007, the American Indian employment rate was 58.2%. The white rate was 63.7%, 5.6 percentage points higher. In the first half of 2009, the American Indian employment rate had fallen to 53.0%. The white rate fell to 60.6%, which made it 7.6 percentage points higher than the American Indian rate. Although both groups have seen employment rate declines, it has been larger for American Indians.

The national data hide considerable variation for American Indians in different regions of the United States. This [report] examines the change in the unemployment rate and employment-to-population ratio for American Indians in eight regions of the country: Alaska, the Midwest, the Northern Plains, the Northeast, the Southern Plains, the Southeast, the Southwest, and the West. Because of the small American Indian sample size by state in the Current Population Survey (the data source for this analysis), it is necessary to combine states into regions to produce reliable statistics. Alaska is the state with, proportionally, the largest Native population (U.S. Census Bureau, 2007). It also has a sample size large enough for a separate analysis.

Alaska Faces Highest Native American Unemployment Rate

Alaskan Natives and American Indians in Alaska experienced consistently high levels of unemployment over the length of the current recession. In the latter half of 2007, when the recession began, the unemployment rate for Alaskan Natives and American Indians in Alaska was 14.8%. This unemployment rate was the highest for all regions in the period. Alaska has not seen any significant increase in the Alaskan Native unemployment rate over the recession. It has only increased to 15.0% in the first half of this year. Nonetheless, this rate is still twice the unemployment rate for whites in Alaska.

The employment-to-population ratio presents a similar picture to the unemployment rate. The native employment rate in Alaska, at 54.4%, was the second lowest of all the regions in the latter half of 2007. As with the unemployment rate, there was little change from the latter half of 2007 to the first half of 2009. The Alaskan Native employment rate was 54.3% in the first half of 2009; the white rate was 66.9%, 12.6 percentage points higher.

Other Double-Digit Unemployment Regions

The Midwest region consists of Arkansas, Illinois, Indiana, Iowa, Michigan, Minnesota, Missouri, Ohio, and Wisconsin. The Midwest saw the second largest increase in the American Indian unemployment rate. In the latter half of 2007, the American Indian unemployment rate in the Midwest was 8.8%. By the first quarter of 2009, it had nearly doubled to 16.5%, making it the region with the second highest unemployment rate. The white unemployment rate in the Midwest doubled, reaching 8.9% in the first half of 2009. This white unemployment rate was slightly more than half the American Indian rate.

The picture from the employment-to-population ratio in the Midwest was somewhat better. In the latter half of 2007, the Midwest had the highest employment rate for American Indians among the eight regions. By the first half of 2009, the American Indian employment rate had declined 5.8 percentage points to 55.6%, dropping the Midwest to the third highest for the regions. The white employment rate decline in the region was smaller, 3.8 percentage points, bringing the white employment rate to 61.4%.

Idaho, Montana, Nebraska, North Dakota, South Dakota, and Wyoming make up the Northern Plains region. In the latter half of 2007, the Northern Plains unemployment rate for American Indians was already in the double digits at 11.1%. This unemployment rate was the second highest among the eight regions. By the first half of 2009, it had increased 4.7 percentage points to a rate of 15.7%.

While the Northern Plains had the second highest American Indian unemployment rate in the latter half of 2007, it had the *lowest* white unemployment rate: 2.6%. The recession has pushed the white unemployment rate up to 5.7% by the first half of 2009, but this rate is still the lowest regional unemployment rate for whites and 10 percentage points lower than the American Indian rate.

The Northern Plains region illustrates the importance of examining the employment-to-population ratio. The increase in unemployment over the recession for American Indians in the Northern Plains at 4.7 percentage points was below the national average for American Indians of 5.8 percentage points.

The decline in employment for American Indians in the Northern Plains, however, was more than twice the national average. The employment rate for American Indians in the Northern Plains declined from 59.2% in the latter half of 2007 to 46.1% in the first half of 2009. In 2009, the Northern Plains had the second-lowest American Indian employment rate. The American Indian employment rate in the Northern Plains declined 13.1 percentage points. Nationally, the employment rate decline was 5.2 percentage points. The employment

American-Indian and White Unemployment Rates by Region 2007 and 2009

American Indian	2007 2nd Half	2009 1st Half	Percentage-Point Change
Alaska	14.8%	15.0%	0.1
Midwest	8.8	16.5	7.6
Northern Plains	11.1	15.7	4.7
Northeast	7.7	12.7	5.1
Southern Plains	6.5	8.9	2.4
Southeast	7.4	10.9	3.5
Southwest	9.2	12.4	3.2
West	6.4	18.7	12.3
White			
Alaska	4.7%	7.4%	2.8
Midwest	4.5	8.9	4.4
Northern Plains	2.6	5.7	3.1
Northeast	3.9	7.2	3.3
Southern Plains	3.7	5.9	2.2
Southeast	3.8	8.4	4.6
Southwest	3.6	7.9	4.3
West	5.2	10.5	5.3

TAKEN FROM: Algernon Austin, *American Indians and the Great Recession*, Economic Policy Institute Issue Brief #264. Washington, DC: EPI, December 7, 2009.

rate indicates that the degree of job loss for American Indians in the Northern Plains is much more severe than the unemployment numbers convey.

While the employment rate declined 13.1 percentage points for Northern Plains American Indians from the latter half of 2007 to the first half of 2009, it only declined 3.5 percentage points for Northern Plains whites. This differential rate of decline in employment means that in the first half of 2009 the American Indian-white employment rate gap is almost 20 percentage points.

Better, but Still Uneven, Unemployment Picture in the Northeast and the South

The Northeast states are Connecticut, Delaware, the District of Columbia, Maine, Maryland, Massachusetts, New Hampshire, New Jersey, New York, Pennsylvania, Rhode Island, and Vermont. In unemployment rates, the Northeast is about average for American Indians. From the latter half of 2007 to the first half of 2009, the unemployment rate increased 5.1 percentage points from 7.7% to 12.7%. In the first half of 2009, the white unemployment rate in the Northeast was 7.2%.

The employment-to-population ratio for American Indians in the Northeast was the third highest in the latter half of 2007. By the first half of 2009, it was the second highest. The shift upward was due to the small decline in employment for Northeast American Indians. The employment rate only declined 1.9 percentage points, falling from 59.5% to 57.6%. The white employment rate fell a similar amount, 2 percentage points, to 61.4%.

The Southern Plains states are Kansas, Oklahoma, and Texas. In terms of unemployment and employment, American Indians in the Southern Plains are currently doing the best. In the first half of 2009, the Southern Plains unemployment rate for American Indians was 8.9%. This was the lowest regional rate for American Indians. Over the recession the Southern Plains unemployment rate has only increased 2.4 percentage points. The white unemployment rate showed a similar increase of 2.2 percentage points, rising to 5.9%.

The perspective from the employment-to-population ratio is also relatively good. In the first half of 2009, the employment rate in the Southern Plains at 58.0% was the highest for American Indians. This rate was up 0.3 percentage points from the start of the recession. In contrast, the white employment rate declined 1.2 percentage points. Nonetheless, in the first half of 2009, the white employment rate was still 4.2 percentage points above the American Indian rate.

Alabama, Florida, Georgia, Kentucky, Louisiana, Mississippi, North Carolina, South Carolina, Tennessee, Virginia, and West Virginia make up the Southeast. American Indians in the Southeast are faring relatively well in comparison with Indians in other regions. Among the eight regions, the Southeast had the second-lowest unemployment rate in the first half of 2009. The rate had increased 3.5 percentage points from the start of the recession to 10.9%, but was smaller than the national-rate increase of 5.8 percentage points. Whites in the Southeast experienced a larger percentage-point rise in unemployment than the American Indians in the region (4.6 percentage points versus 3.5 percentage points), but the white rate of 8.4% in the first half of 2009 was still less than the 10.9% American Indian rate.

Comparing employment-to-population ratios, American Indians in the Southeast are also not faring too badly relative to American Indians in other regions. From the start of the recession to the first half of 2009, the employment rate declined 2.7 percentage points. Nationally, the American Indian employment rate decline was 5.2 percentage points. As with unemployment, whites in the Southeast experienced a larger employment rate drop than American Indians (4 percentage points to 2.7 percentage points). At 57.8%, the white employment rate in the first half of 2009 was 3.3 percentage points higher than the American Indian rate.

The Southwest consists of Arizona, Colorado, Nevada, New Mexico, and Utah. In the latter half of 2007, American Indians in the Southwest had the third-highest unemployment rate among the eight regions. By the first half of 2009, American Indians in the Southwest had the third *lowest* unemployment rate. This shifting of rank was due to the relatively small increase in the American Indian unemployment rate over the recession. The unemployment rate only increased 3.2 percentage points to rise to 12.4% in the first half of 2009. Whites in the region, however, saw a larger increase of 4.3 percentage points, which lifted the white unemployment rate to 7.9%.

Again, the employment-to-population ratio paints a different picture. In the latter half of 2007, American Indians in the Southwest had the lowest employment rate among the eight regions. Over the recession, they have experienced a fairly strong decline in their employment rate of 7.3 percentage points, dropping the rate to 45.0%, which is again the lowest rate regionally for American Indians. The white employment rate declined only 3.9 percentage points in the recession, dropping it to 62.4%.

Worst Unemployment Rate for Native Americans

The states making up the West are California, Hawaii, Oregon, and Washington. Over the recession, the American Indian unemployment rate in the West has gone from being the lowest among American Indians to being the highest. In the latter half of 2007, the American Indian unemployment rate in the West was 6.4%. By the first half of 2009, it had increased 12.3 percentage points to 18.7%. Nearly, one out of every five American Indians in the labor force in the West cannot find work.

Both whites and American Indians in the West have been hit very hard by the recession. But while the American Indian unemployment rate in the West has nearly tripled over the recession, the white unemployment rate has only doubled. In the first half of 2009, the white rate was 10.5%, rising from 5.2% in the last half of 2007.

Although American Indians in the West had the highest unemployment rate in the first half of 2009, they did not have the lowest employment-to-population ratio. At 51.4%, their employment rate was third from the bottom. The size of the employment rate decline was the second largest over the recession. In the first half of 2009, the white employment rate in the West was 59.4%, 8 percentage points above the American Indian rate.

The American Indian-White Regional Disparities

Some regions have fared better economically than others in recent years, and some regions have been hit harder by this recession. One way to begin to assess whether the economic distress among American Indians is merely part of a general regional distress or disproportionate to American Indians is to look at the employment-rate gap between American Indians and whites by region.

[Our data show] that in all dates and regions examined, American Indians had lower employment-to-population ratios than whites. In some regions, the gaps were particularly large. In Alaska, the Northern Plains, and the Southwest, the employment-rate gap was in double digits in the latter half of 2007 *before the start of the recession.* In the Northern Plains, the already large employment-rate gap in 2007 widened 9.6 percentage points by the first half of 2009. In the Northern Plains in the first half of 2009, about 20 percentage points more whites than American Indians were employed. This is an incredibly large disparity. The situation is only slightly better in the Southwest where, in the first half of 2009, the employment-rate gap was 17.4 percentage points.

Worsening Existing Problems

Even before the recession started, the employment-to-population ratios of American Indians were lower than those of whites by region. These gaps were very large in Alaska, the Northern Plains, and the Southwest. These three regions are also the regions of the country where the ratio of the Native-to-non-Native population is among the highest (U.S Census Bureau, 2007). These facts suggest that the problem of low employment rates among American Indians may be at least partially due to conflicts between the two groups. The Great Recession is hurting all groups, but for American Indians, in some areas, it is worsening pre-existing economic disparities.

"Jobs for youth . . . never recovered after the last recession, in 2001."

Teenage Unemployment Is at a Record High

Catherine Rampell

In the viewpoint that follows, Catherine Rampell reports that teenage unemployment in the recent recession has reached a record high—with one out of four teenagers out of work in 2009. She states that the reasons behind the jobless rate are diverse, but include the shortage of jobs available to young workers, the increase in the minimum wage, and the decision of many young people to stay in school. While Rampell acknowledges that the last reason will likely help teenagers to get better paying jobs in the future, she notes that the costs of education demand that many of those young students find work to remain in school. Rampell is an economics editor at the New York Times.

As you read, consider the following questions:

1. According to Rampell, what is Congress doing to help young workers?

2. As Rampell reports, what two working age groups are making it difficult for teenagers to find jobs in the current recession?
3. In Dean Baker's opinion, what is allowing some teenagers to be "pickier about jobs," thus keeping them out of the workforce longer than they were in previous recessions?

Pity the unemployed, but pity especially the young and unemployed.

This August [2009], the teenage unemployment rate—that is, the percentage of teenagers who wanted a job who could not find one—was 25.5 percent, its highest level since the government began keeping track of such statistics in 1948. Likewise, the percentage of teenagers over all who were working was at its lowest level in recorded history.

"There are an amazing number of kids out there looking for work," said Andrew M. Sum, an economics professor at Northeastern University. "And given that unemployment is a lagging indicator, and young people's unemployment even lags behind the rest of unemployment, we're going to see a lot of kids out of work for a long, long, long, long time."

Recessions Disproportionately Hurt the Young

Recessions disproportionately hurt America's youngest and most inexperienced workers, who are often the first to be laid off and the last to be rehired. Jobs for youth also never recovered after the last recession, in 2001.

But this August found more than a quarter of the teenagers in the job market unable to find work, an unemployment rate nearly three times that of the nonteenage population (9 percent), and nearly four times that of workers over 55 (6.8 percent, also a record high for that age group). An estimated 1.64 million people ages 16–19 were unemployed.

Many companies that rely on seasonal business, like leisure and hospitality, held the line and hired fewer workers this summer—a particular problem for teenagers.

In Miami, 18-year-old Rony Bonilla spent past summers busing tables at restaurants and working at the Miami Seaquarium. He said he set out to find another job this summer, but dozens of businesses, like Walgreens, Kmart and Chuck-E-Cheese, turned him down. Mr. Bonilla said he and many of his friends were unable to find any job offers beyond commission-only employment scams.

"I'm looking for anything to pay the bills," he said. "You name it, I applied. And I never even heard from them."

Expecting record unemployment among youth, Congress set aside $1.2 billion in February's [2009] stimulus bill for youth jobs and training. As with everything stimulus-related, supporters, like Jonathan Larsen of the National Youth Employment Coalition, say the money has tempered a bad situation, although the overall numbers are dismal.

Reasons Why Teens Are Unemployed

Economists say there are multiple explanations for why young workers have suffered so much in this downturn, but they mostly boil down to being at the bottom of the totem pole.

Recent college graduates, unable to find higher-paying jobs, are working at places like Starbucks and Gap, taking jobs once held by their younger peers. Half of college graduates under age 25 are in jobs that do not require college degrees, the highest portion in at least 18 years, Mr. Sum said.

Likewise, the reluctance or inability of older workers to retire has led to less attrition and fewer opportunities for workers to move up a rung and make room for new workers at the bottom of the corporate ladder.

Increases in the minimum wage may have made employers reluctant to hire teenagers, said Marvin H. Kosters, a resident scholar emeritus at the American Enterprise Institute.

High teenage jobless rates may also be distorted by other factors. The ability of more young people to rely on family may allow them to be pickier about jobs and therefore to stay out of work longer than they did in previous recessions, said Dean Baker, co-director of the Center for Economic and Policy Research.

Additionally, with more students applying to college, the remaining pool of job applicants may be less desirable to employers.

"Maybe the most employable kids pull out of the labor force, making the numbers for what percent of kids are looking for jobs appear even worse," said Harry J. Holzer, an economist at Georgetown University and the Urban Institute.

Choosing School over Work

The decision of more young people to attend college, which could help them increase their earning potential later in life, may be one silver lining of the recession, economists say. Similarly, back when graduating from high school was a rarer achievement, the Great Depression pushed potential dropouts to stay in high school because work was so hard to come by.

But there is a bit of a catch-22: Many college students need to work to pay for college. Half of traditional-age college students work 20 hours a week, Lawrence F. Katz, an economics professor at Harvard, said.

"In today's labor market, the big margin comes from going on to college, not just graduating high school," he said. "Unlike the decision to finish high school, that's not something you can do free of tuition."

VIEWPOINT 5

"The unemployment rate for older job seekers has more than doubled since 2007 to 7.2 percent in December 2009."

High Unemployment Is Forcing Many Older Workers into Retirement

Emily Brandon

Emily Brandon reports in the following viewpoint that many older Americans are trying to stay in the workforce and delay retirement. Brandon states that seniors have a variety of reasons for wanting to continue working, but many are finding it difficult in the current recession to hold onto jobs or locate new employment opportunities. Brandon asserts that older workers are often the first to be laid off in tough times or are forced into early retirement. They adopt creative ways of lasting through unemployment while finding the right position to meet their needs, Brandon maintains. Emily Brandon writes about retirement and aging in U.S. News & World Report.

As you read, consider the following questions:

1. In November 2009, how long was the average senior jobseeker looking for work, according to Brandon?
2. As Brandon reports, by what percentage did the applications for Social Security benefits surge in 2009?
3. According to the 2009 Employee Benefit Research Institute survey that Brandon cites, how many retirees said they retired before reaching age 65?

Paul Skidmore is hesitant to call himself retired. The former insurance claims adjuster in Finksburg, Md., was laid off in February 2008 and has been job hunting for more than a year. Although at 62 Skidmore is old enough to begin drawing Social Security, he doesn't want to permanently leave the workforce. "On the one hand, my brain is telling me go look for a job," says Skidmore, who originally planned to retire at age 66. "On the other hand, why bother? Just retire."

Skidmore is among a growing number of people who want to work into their 60s but are pushed into early retirement by the weak job market. The number of unemployed Americans ages 55 and older expressing interest in finding a job has grown by 60 percent since the end of 2007, according to the Bureau of Labor Statistics. But finding work has proved difficult. The unemployment rate for older job seekers has more than doubled since 2007 to 7.2 percent in December 2009, and the average duration of the job search for older workers was 36 weeks in November—far longer than the 28 weeks most younger workers remain unemployed. Some discouraged seniors eventually give up on finding a new job and start calling themselves retired.

Trying to Hold onto Jobs in Hard Times

Many workers may want to delay retirement to replenish decimated 401(k) [retirement savings] portfolios, but a larger number may be forced to retire early because of their inability to find new jobs, according to research by Wellesley College economists. The researchers estimate that 378,000 workers will be forced into early retirement in the next five years because of the rising unemployment rate, about 50 percent more people than those who will work longer to recoup stock market losses.

Mike Reimringer, 64, of Rochester, N.Y., once planned to retire at age 70, but he's now among the more than 1.3 million workers ages 55 and older who are employed part time because they have no choice. Two days a week, he works as a quality systems associate for a biological research company. "I am certainly hoping to get bumped up to full time, and I am continuing to job-search," says Reimringer, who was laid off from his last full-time job in December 2008. After a year of looking for full-time employment, he signed up for Social Security benefits in December 2009.

Workers who are at least 62 when they lose their job have the option to sign up for Social Security benefits. The Social Security Administration reported a 21 percent surge in Social Security applications in fiscal year 2009, higher than the 15 percent jump that was expected as the oldest baby boomers reached retirement. The administration's chief actuary, Stephen Goss, attributes the rest of the increase to the weak job market. "This is a gap filler for those people until they can get back to work," he says. "If they don't get back to work, then these benefits will continue for the rest of their lives."

Social Security monthly payments are reduced when they're claimed early. "During the economic downturn, people do start retiring more, and they start doing that at exactly the age at which Social Security becomes available," says Phillip Levine, a Wellesley College economist. "But their Social Security benefits are less than they would have been otherwise." Checks are reduced by 20 to 30 percent for workers who claim benefits at age 62. Those who postpone retirement will see their checks increase by 7 to 8 percent for each year they delay between ages 62 and 70.

Making Ends Meet on Social Security

Although Ellie Naill, 64, would have been eligible for $1,800 a month if she had waited until she turned 66 to claim her benefits, she currently receives just $1,500 each month because she signed up in May 2008—three years earlier than planned. "My husband and I are not making ends meet," says the former real estate agent in Cloverdale, Calif., who retired when her commissions stopped covering her expenses. "I either had to sign up for the money that we could get or we would already be out on the street." Naill now works part time in a fabric store for $10 an hour and is looking for full-time work. "I am cashing in part of my IRA [individual retirement account] to pay our bills for the next few months, hoping a job comes up," she says.

If you reach the average life expectancy, it doesn't matter what age you are when you sign up for Social Security. Retirees who claim their due at 62 receive lower monthly payments for a longer time, while those who delay retirement have higher monthly payments condensed into fewer years. But individuals who live longer than average will come out behind if they claim early. "The risk of taking up Social Security when you are young is you could lock yourself into a lifetime of relatively low retirement benefits," says Richard Johnson, a senior fellow at the Urban Institute. "That's something that could come back to haunt a retiree in their 70s and 80s when their out-of-pocket healthcare costs start going up and they might wish they had an extra $100 or $200 in benefits."

Jim Lord, 63, of Taunton, Mass., calculates that his break-even point is age 77. "If I live past 77, then I should have done it differently," he says. Lord, a former retail design consultant, originally wanted to retire at age 65 but signed up for Social

Security in October 2008 after a layoff. "I didn't have any choice," he says about his early retirement. But Lord admits that he enjoys the extra time for golf and going to the gym.

Retirees who find work again can suspend their Social Security benefits or even repay all of the benefits received and restart their benefits at the higher rate. "It's kind of an interest-free loan," says Reimringer, who plans to try to pay back the Social Security benefits he received and then reclaim at a higher rate at age 70 if he finds a full-time job. "If you're strategic about it, you can use your Social Security benefits like unemployment insurance just to get you over the hump," says Wellesley's Levine. But, he cautions, "very few people who start claiming their Social Security benefits stop claiming them."

This safety net for seniors is a valuable source of emergency income that workers shuttled into an unplanned retirement before age 62 don't have. Philip Staros, 57, claimed his pension and unemployment insurance when he was laid off from MTV networks in December 2008. But that wasn't enough to make his mortgage payments, and his Islip, N.Y., home went to foreclosure. Awaiting the notice to vacate, he works part time for MSG Networks, earning just 40 percent of his former six-figure salary. "I was forced to retire. I took retirement pay to get out of completely starving," he says. "I originally wanted to retire at age 62, the first chance I could collect Social Security."

Staving off Retirement

Most current workers (64 percent) say they plan to retire at age 65 or later or never retire, according to a 2009 Employee Benefit Research Institute [EBRI] survey. But retirement is something that can happen while you are making other plans. Almost half of current retirees left the workforce earlier than their desired retirement age, the survey found. "People want to work longer, but a lot of people find out that they just can't," says Johnson. "Either their health gives out or they can't find a

The Older Workers Who Suffered the Worst Unemployment Rates

As in past years, 2009 unemployment rates were much higher among older African Americans, Hispanics, and workers with limited education than other older workers. Among men age 55 to 64, about 11 percent of Hispanic workers and 10 percent of African American workers were unemployed, compared with 6 percent of non-Hispanic white workers. The unemployment rate for Hispanic men in this age group nearly tripled between 2007 and 2009. At age 65 and older, 2009 male unemployment rates reached about 11 percent for African Americans, 8 percent for Hispanics, and 6 percent for non-Hispanic whites. About 12 percent of male workers age 55 to 64 who did not complete high school were unemployed in 2009, compared with about 5 percent of college graduates. Unemployment did not vary with education as much for workers beyond age 65 as for those a few years younger. The unemployment rate for men age 65 and older who did not complete high school reached only 8.6 percent in 2009, an increase of only 2.4 percentage points since 2007.

Richard W. Johnson and Corina Mommaerts,
How Did Older Workers Fare in 2009?
Urban Institute, March 2010.

job or they lose the job that they have." Some 72 percent of the retirees said they ended up retiring before their 65th birthday. Many of those who retired early said they left the workforce because of a health problem or disability (42 percent), a downsizing or business closure (34 percent), or to care for a spouse or family member (18 percent). Sometimes many of these problems can hit a previously healthy and employed person at the same time.

Deborah Zamudio, 60, retired from her administrative assistant position in June 2009 to care for her husband, who was diagnosed with early-onset dementia. Her unplanned early retirement necessitated major cost-cutting. She downsized from a $1,475 apartment in Milpitas, Calif., to a $540-per-month Utica, N.Y., apartment. "There's no way I could have stayed in California and not worked," she says. "If you have to take early retirement, try to relocate to a less expensive area."

Workers approaching retirement age who are still employed should insulate themselves from job loss as much as possible. "The lower the required skill level and the shorter your tenure is, the more likely it is that you will be the one let go," says Dallas Salisbury, president and chief executive of EBRI. "Keep your training up, and try to build some seniority with an employer." Sometimes, however, a major career change into a more recession-resistant industry is necessary to find work.

After former event planner Jan Albert, 56, of Yorba Linda, Calif., was laid off in August 2007, she took over caregiving responsibilities for her parents. Her mother has Alzheimer's disease, and her father has Parkinson's. She also went back to school to earn a gerontology certification. Albert and her sister then launched an in-home-care business, 24 Hour Angels, which provides elder-care services to 15 clients and employs 20 people. "The baby boomers are going to get old, and there are not enough younger folks to take care of all the elderly," she says. "Anyone who provides services for elders will be in demand."

Making the Right Choices

Those who find new jobs after age 50 typically take pay cuts and give up pension and healthcare benefits, but their second careers often involve less stress and more flexible schedules, according to an Urban Institute and AARP Public Policy Institute study of older workers over a 14-year period. When Jerome Schindler, 67, a Columbus, Ohio, attorney who specializes in food labeling, was laid off from Borden in 1995, he set up his own practice out of his home. He eventually attracted six major clients, including his former employer. "The total income I get from this work isn't as much as I was making at Borden, but it is a more relaxed atmosphere," he says. "I come down to my office in the front room in my pajamas, and I work on the computer." Schindler has recently cut back his working hours to part time and plans to retire fully in 2014.

Early retirement isn't necessarily a bad thing for workers with a pension or enough savings to pay their bills. Many early retirees, even if their retirement was unplanned, say they enjoy the extra time for hobbies and grandchildren. But dreams of world travel have been replaced with renting a *Planet Earth* DVD. And these days, hitting the links means applying for a part-time job at the local golf course.

VIEWPOINT 6

> *"A whole generation of young adults is likely to see its life chances permanently diminished by this recession."*

Unemployment Will Severely Shortchange the Next Generation

Don Peck

In the following viewpoint, Don Peck argues that the recession, which officially began in December 2007 (but has roots that stretch back over a decade of job loss), will have severe consequences for today's youth and subsequent generations. As Peck states, the economy will not likely recover enough to employ all those young people looking for jobs and that unemployment will probably run over 5 percent even in an anticipated period of recovery. Coupled with the lack of opportunities, Peck maintains that young people are also less inclined to seek work in a recession; some, he says, are simply used to their parents solving their problems, while others do not possess the drive to succeed. Regardless, Peck claims that most young workers will likely find themselves stuck in low-paying jobs for some time, having to fight their way up the economic ladder instead of fast-tracking

Don Peck, "How a New Jobless Era Will Transform America," *The Atlantic*, March 2010.

into professional positions. All of these economic strains, Peck asserts, will negatively impact family relationships, marriages, and the rearing of future generations, ultimately reshaping American society. Don Peck is the deputy managing editor of The Atlantic, *the news magazine from which this viewpoint was taken.*

As you read, consider the following questions:

1. How many jobs does America need to produce per month to keep from sinking deeper into joblessness, according to Peck?
2. What two personal problems did sociologist Krysia Mossakowski find were prevalent in young adults who were unemployed for long periods?
3. According to a 2008 Pew survey cited by the author, approximately what percentage of respondents reported that they had not moved forward in life or had actually fallen backward?

How should we characterize the economic period we have now entered? After nearly two brutal years, the Great Recession [the longest economic downturn in the United States of the post-World War II era, officially lasting from December 2007 to June 2009] appears to be over, at least technically. Yet a return to normalcy seems far off. By some measures, each recession since the 1980s has retreated more slowly than the one before it. In one sense, we never fully recovered from the last one, in 2001: the share of the civilian population with a job never returned to its previous peak before this downturn began, and incomes were stagnant throughout the decade. Still, the weakness that lingered through much of the 2000s shouldn't be confused with the trauma of the past two years, a trauma that will remain heavy for quite some time.

The unemployment rate hit 10 percent in October [2009], and there are good reasons to believe that by 2011, 2012, even 2014, it will have declined only a little. Late last year [in 2009], the average duration of unemployment surpassed six months, the first time that has happened since 1948, when the Bureau of Labor Statistics began tracking that number. As of this writing [March 2010], for every open job in the U.S., six people are actively looking for work.

All of these figures understate the magnitude of the jobs crisis. The broadest measure of unemployment and underemployment (which includes people who want to work but have stopped actively searching for a job, along with those who want full-time jobs but can find only part-time work) reached 17.4 percent in October, which appears to be the highest figure since the 1930s. And for large swaths of society—young adults, men, minorities—that figure was much higher (among teenagers, for instance, even the narrowest measure of unemployment stood at roughly 27 percent). One recent survey showed that 44 percent of families had experienced a job loss, a reduction in hours, or a pay cut in the past year.

The New Era of High Unemployment

There is unemployment, a brief and relatively routine transitional state that results from the rise and fall of companies in any economy, and there is *unemployment*—chronic, all-consuming. The former is a necessary lubricant in any engine of economic growth. The latter is a pestilence that slowly eats away at people, families, and, if it spreads widely enough, the fabric of society. Indeed, history suggests that it is perhaps society's most noxious ill.

The worst effects of pervasive joblessness—on family, politics, society—take time to incubate, and they show themselves only slowly. But ultimately, they leave deep marks that endure long after boom times have returned. Some of these marks are just now becoming visible, and even if the economy magically and fully recovers tomorrow, new ones will continue to appear. The longer our economic slump lasts, the deeper they'll be.

If it persists much longer, this era of high joblessness will likely change the life course and character of a generation of young adults—and quite possibly those of the children behind them as well. It will leave an indelible imprint on many blue-collar white men—and on white culture. It could change the nature of modern marriage, and also cripple marriage as an institution in many communities. It may already be plunging many inner cities into a kind of despair and dysfunction not seen for decades. Ultimately, it is likely to warp our politics, our culture, and the character of our society for years. . . .

The economy now sits in a hole more than 10 million jobs deep—that's the number required to get back to 5 percent unemployment, the rate we had before the recession started, and one that's been more or less typical for a generation. And because the population is growing and new people are continually coming onto the job market, we need to produce roughly 1.5 million new jobs a year—about 125,000 a month—just to keep from sinking deeper.

Even if the economy were to immediately begin producing 600,000 jobs a month—more than double the pace of the mid-to-late 1990s, when job growth was strong—it would take roughly two years to dig ourselves out of the hole we're in. The economy could add jobs that fast, or even faster—job growth is theoretically limited only by labor supply, and a lot more labor is sitting idle today than usual. But the U.S. hasn't seen that pace of sustained employment growth in more than 30 years. And given the particulars of this recession, matching idle workers with new jobs—even once economic growth picks up—seems likely to be a particularly slow and challenging process.

The construction and finance industries, bloated by a decade-long housing bubble, are unlikely to regain their former share of the economy, and as a result many out-of-work finance professionals and construction workers won't be able to simply pick up where they left off when growth returns—they'll need to retrain and find new careers. (For different reasons, the same might be said of many media professionals and auto workers.) And even within industries that are likely to bounce back smartly, temporary layoffs have generally given way to the permanent elimination of jobs, the result of workplace restructuring. Manufacturing jobs have of course been moving overseas for decades, and still are; but recently, the outsourcing of much white-collar work has become possible. Companies that have cut domestic payrolls to the bone in this recession may choose to rebuild them in Shanghai, Guangzhou, or Bangalore, accelerating off-shoring decisions that otherwise might have occurred over many years.

The Economy After Recovery

New jobs will come open in the U.S. But many will have different skill requirements than the old ones. "In a sense," says Gary Burtless, a labor economist at the Brookings Institution, "every time someone's laid off now, they need to start all over. They don't even know what industry they'll be in next." And as a spell of unemployment lengthens, skills erode and behavior tends to change, leaving some people unqualified even for work they once did well.

Ultimately, innovation is what allows an economy to grow quickly and create new jobs as old ones obsolesce and disappear. Typically, one salutary side effect of recessions is that they eventually spur booms in innovation. Some laid-off employees become entrepreneurs, working on ideas that have been ignored by corporate bureaucracies, while sclerotic firms in declining industries fail, making way for nimbler enterprises. But according to the economist Edmund Phelps, the innovative potential of the U.S. economy looks limited today. In a recent *Harvard Business Review* article, he and his co-author, Leo Tilman, argue that dynamism in the U.S. has actually been in decline for a decade; with the housing bubble fueling easy (but unsustainable) growth for much of that time, we just didn't notice. Phelps and Tilman finger several culprits: a patent system that's become stifling; an increasingly myopic focus among public companies on quarterly results, rather than long-term value creation; and, not least, a financial industry that for a generation has focused its talent and resources not on funding business innovation, but on proprietary trading, regulatory arbitrage, and arcane financial engineering. None of these problems is likely to disappear quickly. Phelps, who won a Nobel Prize for his work on the "natural" rate of unemployment, believes that until they do disappear, the new floor for unemployment is likely to be between 6.5 percent and 7.5 percent, even once "recovery" is complete.

It's likely, then, that for the next several years or more, the jobs environment will more closely resemble today's environment than that of 2006 or 2007—or for that matter, the environment to which we were accustomed for a generation. Heidi Shierholz, an economist at the Economic Policy Institute, notes that if the recovery follows the same basic path as the last two (in 1991 and 2001), unemployment will stand at roughly 8 percent in 2014.

"We haven't seen anything like this before: a really deep recession combined with a really extended period, maybe as much as eight years, all told, of highly elevated unemployment," Shierholz told me. "We're about to see a big national experiment on stress."

Young People Are Trying to Stay Positive

"I'm definitely seeing a lot of the older generation saying, 'Oh, this [recession] is so awful,'" Robert Sherman, a 2009 graduate of Syracuse University, told *The New York Times* in July. "But my generation isn't getting as depressed and uptight." Sherman had recently turned down a $50,000-a-year job at a consulting firm, after careful deliberation with his parents, because he hadn't connected well with his potential bosses.

Instead he was doing odd jobs and trying to get a couple of tech companies off the ground. "The economy will rebound," he said.

Over the past two generations, particularly among many college grads, the 20s have become a sort of netherworld between adolescence and adulthood. Job-switching is common, and with it, periods of voluntary, transitional unemployment. And as marriage and parenthood have receded farther into the future, the first years after college have become, arguably, more carefree. In this recession, the term *funemployment* has gained some currency among single 20-somethings, prompting a small raft of youth-culture stories in the *Los Angeles Times* and *San Francisco Weekly*, on [blog] Gawker, and in other venues.

Most of the people interviewed in these stories seem merely to be trying to stay positive and make the best of a bad situation. They note that it's a good time to reevaluate career choices; that since joblessness is now so common among their peers, it has lost much of its stigma; and that since they don't have mortgages or kids, they have flexibility, and in this respect, they are lucky. All of this sounds sensible enough—it is intuitive to think that youth will be spared the worst of the recession's scars.

But in fact a whole generation of young adults is likely to see its life chances permanently diminished by this recession. Lisa Kahn, an economist at Yale, has studied the impact of recessions on the lifetime earnings of young workers. In one recent study, she followed the career paths of white men who graduated from college between 1979 and 1989. She found that, all else equal, for every one-percentage-point increase in the national unemployment rate, the starting income of new graduates fell by as much as 7 percent; the unluckiest graduates of the decade, who emerged into the teeth of the 1981–82 recession, made roughly 25 percent less in their first year than graduates who stepped into boom times.

But what's truly remarkable is the persistence of the earnings gap. Five, 10, 15 years after graduation, after untold promotions and career changes spanning booms and busts, the unlucky graduates never closed the gap. Seventeen years after graduation, those who had entered the workforce during inhospitable times were still earning 10 percent less on average than those who had emerged into a more bountiful climate. When you add up all the earnings losses over the years, Kahn says, it's as if the lucky graduates had been given a gift of about $100,000, adjusted for inflation, immediately upon graduation—or, alternatively, as if the unlucky ones had been saddled with a debt of the same size.

When Kahn looked more closely at the unlucky graduates at mid-career, she found some surprising characteristics. They were significantly less likely to work in professional occupations or other prestigious spheres. And they clung more tightly to their jobs: average job tenure was unusually long. People who entered the workforce during the recession "didn't switch jobs as much, and particularly for young workers, that's how you increase wages," Kahn told me. This behavior may have resulted from a lingering risk aversion, born of a tough start. But a lack of opportunities may have played a larger role, she said: when you're forced to start work in a particularly low-level job or unsexy career, it's easy for other employers to dismiss you as having low potential. Moving up, or moving on to something different and better, becomes more difficult.

The Disappearance of Fast-Track Jobs

"Graduates' first jobs have an inordinate impact on their career path and [lifetime earnings]," wrote Austan Goolsbee, now a member of President [Barack] Obama's Council of Economic Advisers, in *The New York Times* in 2006. "People essentially cannot close the wage gap by working their way up the company hierarchy. While they may work their way up, the people who started above them do, too. They don't catch up." Recent research suggests that as much as two-thirds of real lifetime wage growth typically occurs in the first 10 years of a career. After that, as people start families and their career paths lengthen and solidify, jumping the tracks becomes harder.

This job environment is not one in which fast-track jobs are plentiful, to say the least. According to the National Association of Colleges and Employers, job offers to graduating seniors declined 21 percent last year, and are expected to decline another 7 percent this year. Last spring, in the San Francisco Bay Area, an organization called JobNob began holding networking happy hours to try to match college graduates with start-up companies looking primarily for unpaid labor. Julie Greenberg, a co-founder of JobNob, says that at the first event, on May 7, she expected perhaps 30 people, but 300 showed up. New graduates didn't have much of a chance; most of the people there had several years of work experience—quite a lot were 30-somethings—and some had more than one degree. JobNob has since held events for alumni of Stanford, Berkeley, and Harvard; all have been well attended (at the Harvard event, Greenberg tried to restrict attendance to 75, but about 100 people managed to get in), and all have been dominated by people with significant work experience.

When experienced workers holding prestigious degrees are taking unpaid internships, not much is left for newly minted B.A.s [college graduates with Bachelor of Arts degrees]. Yet if those same B.A.s don't find purchase in the job market, they'll soon have to compete with a fresh class of graduates—ones without white space on their résumé to explain. This is a tough squeeze to escape, and it only gets tighter over time.

The Psychological Impact of Joblessness

Strong evidence suggests that people who don't find solid roots in the job market within a year or two have a particularly hard time righting themselves. In part, that's because many of them become different—and damaged—people. Krysia Mossakowski, a sociologist at the University of Miami, has found that in young adults, long bouts of unemployment provoke long-lasting changes in behavior and mental health. "Some people say, 'Oh, well, they're young, they're in and out of the workforce, so unemployment shouldn't matter much psychologically,'" Mossakowski told me. "But that isn't true."

Examining national longitudinal data, Mossakowski has found that people who were unemployed for long periods in their teens or early 20s are far more likely to develop a habit of heavy drinking (five or more drinks in one sitting) by the time they approach middle age. They are also more likely to develop depressive symptoms. Prior drinking behavior and psychological history do not explain these problems—they result from unemployment itself. And the problems are not limited to those who never find steady work; they show up quite strongly as well in people who are later working regularly.

Forty years ago, Glen Elder, a sociologist at the University of North Carolina and a pioneer in the field of "life course" studies, found a pronounced diffidence in elderly men (though not women) who had suffered hardship as 20- and 30-somethings during the Depression. Decades later, unlike peers who had been largely spared in the 1930s, these men came across, he told me, as "beaten and withdrawn—lacking ambition, direction, confidence in themselves." Today in Japan, according to the Japan Productivity Center for Socio-Economic Development, workers who began their careers during the "lost decade" of the 1990s and are now in their 30s make up six out of every 10 cases of depression, stress, and work-related mental disabilities reported by employers.

A large and long-standing body of research shows that physical health tends to deteriorate during unemployment, most likely through a combination of fewer financial resources and a higher stress level. The most-recent research suggests that poor health is prevalent among the young, and endures for a lifetime. Till Von Wachter, an economist at Columbia University, and Daniel Sullivan, of the Federal Reserve Bank of Chicago, recently looked at the mortality rates of men who had lost their jobs in Pennsylvania in the 1970s and '80s. They found that particularly among men in their 40s or 50s, mortality rates rose markedly soon after a layoff. But regardless of age, all men were left with an elevated risk of dying in each year following their episode of unemployment, for the rest of their lives. And so, the younger the worker, the more pronounced the effect on his lifespan: the lives of workers who had lost their job at 30, Von Wachter and Sullivan found, were shorter than those who had lost their job at 50 or 55—and more than a year and a half shorter than those who'd never lost their job at all.

Generation Me

Journalists and academics have thrown various labels at today's young adults, hoping one might stick—Generation Y, Generation Next, the Net Generation, the Millennials, the Echo Boomers. All of these efforts contain an element of folly; the diversity of character within a generation is always and infinitely larger than the gap between generations. Still, the cultural and economic environment in which each generation is incubated clearly matters. It is no coincidence that the members of Generation X—painted as cynical, apathetic slackers—first emerged into the workforce in the weak job market of the early-to-mid-1980s. Nor is it a coincidence that the early members of Generation Y—labeled as optimistic, rule-following achievers—came of age during the Internet boom of the late 1990s.

Many of today's young adults seem temperamentally unprepared for the circumstances in which they now find themselves. Jean Twenge, an associate professor of psychology at San Diego State University, has carefully compared the attitudes of today's young adults to those of previous generations when they were the same age. Using national survey data, she's found that to an unprecedented degree, people who graduated from high school in the 2000s dislike the idea of work for work's sake, and expect jobs and career to be tailored to their interests and lifestyle. Yet they also have much higher material expectations than previous generations, and believe financial success is extremely important. "There's this idea that, 'Yeah, I don't want to work, but I'm still going to get all the stuff I want,'" Twenge told me. "It's a generation in which every kid has been told, 'You can be anything you want. You're special.'"

In her 2006 book, *Generation Me*, Twenge notes that self-esteem in children began rising sharply around 1980, and hasn't stopped since. By 1999, according to one survey, 91 percent of teens described themselves as responsible, 74 percent as physically attractive, and 79 percent as very intelligent. (More than 40 percent of teens also expected that they would be earning $75,000 a year or more by age 30; the median salary made by a 30-year-old was $27,000 that year.) Twenge attributes the shift to broad changes in parenting styles and teaching methods, in response to the growing belief that children should always feel good about themselves, no matter what. As the years have passed, efforts to boost self-esteem—and to decouple it from performance—have become widespread.

These efforts have succeeded in making today's youth more confident and individualistic. But that may not benefit them in adulthood, particularly in this economic environment. Twenge writes that "self-esteem without basis encourages laziness rather than hard work," and that "the ability to persevere and keep going" is "a much better predictor of life outcomes than self-esteem." She worries that many young people might be inclined to simply give up in this job market. "You'd think if people are more individualistic, they'd be more independent," she told me. "But it's not really true. There's an element of entitlement—they expect people to figure things out for them."

A Lack of Perseverance and Independence Among the Young

Ron Alsop, a former reporter for *The Wall Street Journal* and the author of *The Trophy Kids Grow Up: How the Millennial Generation Is Shaking Up the Workplace*, says a combination of entitlement and highly structured childhood has resulted in a lack of independence and entrepreneurialism in many 20-somethings. They're used to checklists, he says, and "don't excel at leadership or independent problem solving." Alsop interviewed dozens of employers for his book, and concluded that unlike previous generations, Millennials, as a group, "need almost constant direction" in the workplace. "Many flounder without precise guidelines but thrive in structured situations that provide clearly defined rules."

All of these characteristics are worrisome, given a harsh economic environment that requires perseverance, adaptability, humility, and entrepreneurialism. Perhaps most worrisome, though, is the fatalism and lack of agency that both Twenge and Alsop discern in today's young adults. Trained throughout childhood to disconnect performance from reward, and told repeatedly that they are destined for great things, many are quick to place blame elsewhere when something goes wrong, and are inclined to believe that bad situations will sort themselves out—or will be sorted out by parents or other helpers. . . .

According to a recent Pew [Research Center] survey, 10 percent of adults younger than 35 have moved back in with their parents as a result of the recession. But that's merely an acceleration of a trend that has been under way for a generation or more. By the middle of the aughts, for instance, the percentage of 26-year-olds living with their parents reached 20 percent, nearly double what it was in 1970. Well before the recession began, this generation of young adults was less likely to work, or at least work steadily, than other recent generations. Since 2000, the percentage of people age 16 to 24 participating in the labor force has been declining (from 66 percent to 56 percent across the decade). Increased college attendance explains only part of the shift; the rest is a puzzle. Lingering weakness in the job market since 2001 may be one cause. Twenge believes the propensity of this generation to pursue "dream" careers that are, for most people, unlikely to work out may also be partly responsible. (In 2004, a national survey found that about one out of 18 college freshmen expected to make a living as an actor, musician, or artist.)

Whatever the reason, the fact that so many young adults weren't firmly rooted in the workforce even before the crash is deeply worrying. It means that a very large number of young adults entered the recession already vulnerable to all the ills that joblessness produces over time. It means that for a sizeable proportion of 20- and 30-somethings, the next few years will likely be toxic. . . .

Looking for a Silver Lining

No one tries harder than the jobless to find silver linings in this national economic disaster. Many of the people I spoke with for this story said that unemployment, while extremely painful, had improved them in some ways: they'd become less materialistic and more financially prudent; they were using free time to volunteer more, and were enjoying that; they were more empathetic now, they said, and more aware of the struggles of others.

In limited respects, perhaps the recession will leave society better off. At the very least, it's awoken us from our national fever dream of easy riches and bigger houses, and put a necessary end to an era of reckless personal spending. Perhaps it will leave us humbler, and gentler toward one another, too—at least in the long run. A recent paper by the economists Paola Giuliano and Antonio Spilimbergo shows that generations that endured a recession in early adulthood became more concerned about inequality and more cognizant of the role luck plays in life. And in his book, *Children of the Great Depression*, Glen Elder wrote that adolescents who experienced hardship in the 1930s became especially adaptable, family-oriented adults; perhaps, as a result of this recession, today's adolescents will be pampered less and counted on for more, and will grow into adults who feel less entitled than recent generations.

But for the most part, these benefits seem thin, uncertain, and far off. In *The Moral Consequences of Economic Growth*, the economic historian Benjamin Friedman argues that both inside and outside the U.S., lengthy periods of economic stagnation or decline have almost always left society more mean-spirited and less inclusive, and have usually stopped or reversed the advance of rights and freedoms. A high level of national wealth, Friedman writes, "is no bar to a society's retreat into rigidity and intolerance once enough of its citizens lose the sense that they are getting ahead." When material progress falters, Friedman concludes, people become more jealous of their status relative to others. Anti-immigrant sentiment typically increases, as does conflict between races and classes; concern for the poor tends to decline.

Social forces take time to grow strong, and time to dissipate again. Friedman told me that the phenomenon he's studied "is not about business cycles . . . It's not about people comparing where they are now to where they were a year ago." The relevant comparisons are much broader: What opportunities are available to me, relative to those of my parents? What opportunities do my children have? What is the trajectory of my career?

It's been only about two years since this most recent recession started, but then again, most people hadn't been getting ahead for a decade. In a Pew survey in the spring of 2008, more than half of all respondents said that over the past five years, they either hadn't moved forward in life or had actually fallen backward, the most downbeat assessment that either Pew or Gallup has ever recorded, in nearly a half century of polling. Median household income in 2008 was the lowest since 1997, adjusting for inflation. "On the latest income data," Friedman said, "we're 11 years into a period of decline." By the time we get out of the current downturn, we'll likely be "up to a decade and a half. And that's surely enough."

Income inequality usually falls during a recession, and the economist and happiness expert Andrew Clark says that trend typically provides some emotional salve to the poor and the middle class. (Surveys, lab experiments, and brain readings all show that, for better or worse, schadenfreude [happiness derived from others' misfortune] is a powerful psychological force: at any fixed level of income, people are happier when the income of others is reduced.) But income inequality hasn't shrunk in this recession. In 2007–08, the most recent year for which data is available, it widened.

Indeed, this period of economic weakness may reinforce class divides, and decrease opportunities to cross them—especially for young people. The research of Till Von Wachter, the economist at Columbia University, suggests that not all people graduating into a recession see their life chances dimmed: those with degrees from elite universities catch up fairly quickly to where they otherwise would have been if they'd graduated in better times; it's the masses beneath them that are left behind. Princeton's 2009 graduating class found more jobs in financial services than in any other industry. According to Princeton's career-services director, Beverly Hamilton-Chandler, campus visits and hiring by the big investment banks have been down, but that decline has been partly offset by an uptick in recruiting by hedge funds and boutique financial firms.

The Seeds of Discontent

In the Internet age, it is particularly easy to see the bile that has always lurked within American society. More difficult, in the moment, is discerning precisely how these lean times are affecting society's character. In many respects, the U.S. was more socially tolerant entering this recession than at any time in its history, and a variety of national polls on social conflict since then have shown mixed results. Signs of looming class warfare or racial conflagration are not much in evidence. But some seeds of discontent are slowly germinating. The town-hall meetings last summer and fall were contentious, often uncivil, and at times given over to inchoate outrage. *One National Journal* poll in October [2009] showed that whites (especially white men) were feeling particularly anxious about their future and alienated by the government. We will have to wait and see exactly how these hard times will reshape our social fabric. But they certainly will reshape it, and all the more so the longer they extend.

Periodical Bibliography

The following articles have been selected to supplement the diverse views presented in this chapter.

America	"No Bailout for Teens," June 7, 2010.
Tamara Audi	"Bypassed by the Recovery," *Wall Street Journal*, June 17, 2010.
Ronald Brownstein	"Trend Lines Favor Working Women," *National Journal*, June 19, 2010.
Current Events	"Help Not Wanted," February 22, 2010.
Mark Dolliver	"Hello, Dad, I'm Back!" *MediaWeek*, May 17, 2010.
Kevin A. Hassett	"Racial Recession," *National Review*, March 22, 2010.
Michael McKee	"In this Recovery, Small Business Falls Behind," *BusinessWeek*, February 22, 2010.
Rachel Mendleson	"When Reality Bites," *Maclean's*, April 12, 2010.
Zaid Shakir	"Graveyard Detroit," *Tikkun*, May/June 2010.
Alina Tugend	"What Recovery? For the Unemployed, the Pain Gets Worse," *New York Times*, July 3, 2010.
George F. Will	"The Basement Boys," *Newsweek*, March 8, 2010.

Chapter 3

How Effective Is the Government's Response to Unemployment?

Chapter Preface

On February 17, 2009, President Barack Obama signed the American Recovery and Reinvestment Act of 2009 (ARRA) into law. The act, which had passed Congress only a week before, created $787 billion in tax cuts and spending provisions for welfare, education, and health care in hopes of shoring up the declining business performance and resulting widespread unemployment that followed the 2007 financial crisis. Besides increasing the safety net for the millions of unemployed Americans, the ARRA stimulus package put money into federal projects (such as highway and bridge construction and the expansion of mass transit and alternative energy) that would ostensibly employ hundreds of thousands of workers. On September 2 of that year, Deborah Solomon claimed in the *Wall Street Journal*, "Economists say the money out the door—combined with the expectation of additional funds flowing soon—is fueling growth above where it would have been without any government action."

Not every observer agrees with such an optimistic assessment, and, as arguments in the following chapter confirm, experts are certainly not united in viewing the impact of the stimulus upon unemployment so positively. However, even if job growth has occurred, not all analysts are convinced the stimulus is enough. *Mother Jones* Washington, D.C., bureau chief David Corn wondered in a July 2, 2010, blog posting what President Obama can do since the passage of the ARRA to compensate for the 8 million jobs lost over the last two years. Corn asks, "How long can Obama and his crew keep saying the same thing: the recovery is weak, but we're doing the best we can?" Steve Kornacki, writing on the same day for Salon.com, stated sourly, "Today, we are told, the actual recession is probably over, and the rapid growth in the unemployment rate actually stopped months ago. For most of 2010, it has held steady in the 9.7 percent range, with no signs of a steep drop on the horizon. Yes, the 9.5 percent figure reported today is the lowest mark in a year, but it's largely a function of hundreds of thousands of unemployed Americans giving up the job hunt." Both Corn and Kornacki—as well as other critics of the administration—point out that the private sector is still not creating enough jobs per month to employ new entrants into the job market let alone the millions who have been out of work for months. They insist Obama's leadership is failing to inspire confidence among business leaders or among the legions of unemployed. A June 2010 NBC/*Wall Street Journal* poll indicated that the President's approval rating had dropped to 45 percent, while 48 percent of those polled disapproved of his performance.

David Leonhardt of the *New York Times* believes critics have misled the public about the impact of the stimulus program and its lasting effects. Writing on February 16, 2010, Leonhardt asserts that three reputable and impartial sources "estimate that the bill has added 1.6 million to 1.8 million jobs so far and that its ultimate impact will be roughly 2.5 million jobs." Leonhardt agrees the national work projects have not taken off as promised, but he maintains the aid to cities across the country has had positive results. Mayor Phil Gordon of Phoenix, Arizona, is just one city official who agrees. In a special report to CNN on January 25, 2010, Gordon extolled the $11.7 million award the city received from ARRA to reconstruct an airport taxiway and additional funds Phoenix garnered to save teaching positions and help put people to work weatherizing homes. Since these projects are ongoing, Leonhardt's and Gordon's testimonies suggest the stimulus is still working even if its overall impacts cannot immediately counteract the country's staggering unemployment.

In the following chapter, various experts and pundits share their views on the government's job-creation plan and the administration's claims that the worst of the economic crisis is over.

"Recipients [of government stimulus money] reported that ARRA funded almost 700,000 full-time-equivalent (FTE) jobs during the first quarter of 2010."

The Economic Stimulus Plan Is Reducing Unemployment

Congressional Budget Office

In the following viewpoint, the Congressional Budget Office (CBO) claims that the American Recovery and Reinvestment Act of 2009 (ARRA) has been successful in creating jobs. The ARRA was designed by the administration of President Barack Obama and passed by Congress. The intent of the act is to stimulate the flagging economy, in part, through government grants and loans to businesses. Recipients are to use the money to create jobs, and these companies must then prove to the government that new positions have been added and filled. The CBO maintains that recipient businesses have created more than 700,000 jobs with

Congressional Budget Office, *Estimated Impact of the American Recovery and Reinvestment Act on Employment and Economic Output from January 2010 Through March 2010.* Washington, DC: Congressional Budget Office, May 2010.

stimulus money and lowered the national unemployment rate in the first quarter of 2010. The CBO is an agency mandated to provide Congress with fiscal information pertaining to the national budget.

As you read, consider the following questions:

1. According to the CBO, how much has the gross domestic product (GDP) been raised by the government's stimulus package?
2. By how much, according to the viewpoint, has the ARRA increased the number of employed persons in the United States?
3. What does the CBO expect will happen to the impact of the ARRA in 2011?

Under the American Recovery and Reinvestment Act of 2009 (ARRA), also known as the economic stimulus package, certain recipients of funds appropriated in ARRA (most grant and loan recipients, contractors, and subcontractors) are required to report, after the end of each calendar quarter, the number of jobs they created or retained with ARRA funding. The law also requires the Congressional Budget Office (CBO) to comment on those reported numbers.

Recipients reported that ARRA funded almost 700,000 full-time-equivalent (FTE) jobs during the first quarter of 2010. Such reports, however, do not provide a comprehensive estimate of the law's impact on employment in the United States. That impact may be higher or lower than the reported number for several reasons (in addition to any issues about the quality of the data in the reports). First, some of the reported jobs might have existed in the absence of the stimulus package, with employees working on the same activities or other activities. Second, the reports filed by recipients measure only the jobs created by employers who received ARRA funding directly or by their immediate subcontractors (so-called

Estimated Macroeconomic Impact of the American Recovery and Reinvestment Act, 2009 to 2012

	Change Attributable to ARRA							
	Real Gross Domestic Product (Percent)		Unemployment Rate (Percentage Points)		Employment (Millions of People)		Full-Time-Equivalent Employment (Millions)[a]	
	Low Estimate	High Estimate	Low Estimate	High Estimate	Low Estimate	High Estimate	Low Estimate	High Estimate
2009 (Calendar Year Quarter)								
Q1	0.1	0.1	*	*	*	*	*	0.1
Q2	0.9	1.5	-0.2	-0.3	0.3	0.5	0.5	0.8
Q3	1.3	2.7	-0.4	-0.7	0.7	1.3	1.0	1.9
Q4	1.5	3.5	-0.5	-1.1	1.0	2.1	1.4	3.0
2010 (Calendar Year Quarter)								
Q1	1.7	4.2	-0.7	-1.5	1.2	2.8	1.8	4.1
Q2	1.7	4.6	-0.8	-1.9	1.4	3.4	2.0	4.9
Q3	1.4	4.2	-0.8	-2.0	1.4	3.7	2.0	5.3
Q4	1.1	3.6	-0.7	-1.9	1.3	3.6	1.8	5.1

continued

Estimated Macroeconomic Impact of the American Recovery and Reinvestment Act, 2009 to 2012

[CONTINUED]

	Change Attributable to ARRA							
	Real Gross Domestic Product (Percent)		Unemployment Rate (Percentage points)		Employment (Millions of people)		Full-Time-Equivalent Employment (Millions)[a]	
	Low Estimate	High Estimate	Low Estimate	High Estimate	Low Estimate	High Estimate	Low Estimate	High Estimate
Calendar Year Average								
2009	1.0	2.0	-0.3	-0.5	0.5	1.0	0.7	1.4
2010	1.5	4.2	-0.7	-1.8	1.3	3.4	1.9	4.8
2011	0.7	2.2	-0.5	-1.4	0.9	2.6	1.2	3.6
2012	0.1	0.3	-0.1	-0.4	0.2	0.7	0.2	0.7

Note: * = Between -0.05 and 0.05.

[a]A year of full-time-equivalent employment is 40 hours of employment per week for one year.

TAKEN FROM: CBO, *Estimated Impact of the American Recovery and Reinvestment Act on Employment and Economic Output from January 2010 Through March 2010*. Washington, DC: CBO, May 2010.

primary and secondary recipients), not by lower-level subcontractors. Third, the reports do not attempt to measure the number of jobs that may have been created or retained indirectly, as greater income for recipients and their employees boosted demand for products and services. Fourth, the recipients' reports cover only certain appropriations made in ARRA, which encompass about one-sixth of the total amount spent by the government or conveyed through tax reductions in ARRA during the first quarter; the reports do not measure the effects of other provisions of the stimulus package, such as tax cuts and transfer payments (including unemployment insurance payments) to individuals.

Benefits of the Stimulus Package

Estimating the law's overall effects on employment requires a more comprehensive analysis than the recipients' reports provide. Therefore, looking at recorded spending to date as well as estimates of the other effects of ARRA on spending and revenues, CBO has estimated the law's impact on employment and economic output using evidence about the effects of previous similar policies on the economy and using various mathematical models that represent the workings of the economy. On that basis, CBO estimates that in the first quarter of calendar year 2010, ARRA's policies:

- Raised the level of real (inflation-adjusted) gross domestic product (GDP) by between 1.7 percent and 4.2 percent,
- Lowered the unemployment rate by between 0.7 percentage points and 1.5 percentage points,
- Increased the number of people employed by between 1.2 million and 2.8 million, and
- Increased the number of full-time-equivalent jobs by 1.8 million to 4.1 million compared with what those

> amounts would have been otherwise. (Increases in FTE jobs include shifts from part-time to full-time work or overtime and are thus generally larger than increases in the number of employed workers.)

The effects of ARRA on output and employment are expected to increase further during calendar year 2010 but then diminish in 2011 and fade away by the end of 2012.

CBO's current estimates reflect small revisions to earlier projections of the timing and magnitude of changes to federal spending and revenues under ARRA and small revisions to the estimated impact of changes in spending and revenues on GDP and employment.

CBO has examined data on output and employment during the period since ARRA's enactment. However, those data are not as helpful in determining ARRA's economic effects as might be supposed, because isolating those effects would require knowing what path the economy would have taken in the absence of the law. Because that path cannot be observed, the new data add only limited information about ARRA's impact.

VIEWPOINT 2

> *"Canceling the job-destroying 'stimulus' program would be a good first step toward providing the private sector with the additional capital required to achieve full employment."*

The Economic Stimulus Plan Is Increasing Unemployment

Louis Woodhill

In response to the financial crisis that began in late 2007, President Barack Obama urged Congress to pass the American Recovery and Reinvestment Act of 2009 (ARRA). Once the measure became law, the government distributed $787 billion to businesses in an effort to salvage hard-hit industries and encourage them to create new jobs to decrease staggering unemployment levels. In the viewpoint that follows, Louis Woodhill argues that the economic stimulus plan has not lived up to its promises. According to Woodhill, job loss is accelerating after the plan's implementation primarily because the private sector has had to fund the stimulus package instead of growing jobs. With business money now tied up in federal bonds to pay for the stimulus, Woodhill claims these companies cannot afford to reverse the process without creating more unemployment. Louis Woodhill is *an engineer and software entrepreneur who is a member of the Leadership Council of the Club for Growth, a conservative advocacy organization that seeks to elect pro-growth candidates to public office.*

As you read, consider the following questions:

1. As Woodhill states, when the gross domestic product (GDP) grew by 3.5 percent in the third quarter of 2009, how many jobs were lost in the same period?
2. In what part of the business sector does most new job growth occur, according to Woodhill?
3. What two measures does Woodhill suggest would be more effective than further government stimulus in increasing incentives for savings and investment?

"Stimulus" is in the process of turning a nasty recession into a genuine depression. The evidence is in the "Employment Situation" report released by the Bureau of Labor Statistics (BLS) on November 6th [2009]. The "headline" unemployment rate shot up to 10.2%, the highest in more than 26 years. But the report was much worse than most people realize.

The "household survey data" showed that 589,000 jobs vanished during October. This is bad enough, but the three-month moving average of changes in total employment (current month and prior two months) shows that job losses are actually *accelerating*.

The three-month moving average (TMMA) of changes in total employment began a serious decline in February 2007. It went into negative territory two months later. This indicator has now been negative for the past 21 months. During this time, total employment has declined by more than 8 million jobs.

As the financial crisis gathered momentum in late 2008, the TMMA fell continuously, reaching a bottom of 853,000 jobs lost per month in January 2009. Then this indicator began improving. By June 2009, when stories about "green shoots" [any sign of growth or recovery] were common in the financial press, the TMMA was "only" 230,000. However, it then began falling again. The October BLS numbers pushed the TMMA down to 589,000 jobs lost per month.

Shedding More Jobs than Were Created

Economic growth is supposed to *create* jobs. However, the U.S. economy shed twice as many jobs (1,332,000) in the third quarter of 2009, when GDP [gross domestic product] grew at a robust 3.5% annual rate, than it did in the second quarter (691,000), when the economy contracted at a 0.7% rate.

How can this be? To paraphrase the 1992 [Bill] Clinton [presidential] campaign, "It's the bonds, stupid!"

The massive sales of U.S. Treasury bonds to finance "stimulus", bailouts, and other government spending is sucking capital out of the private sector and destroying jobs. Once again, the October 6th BLS report tells the tale.

The BLS "household survey" showed job losses of 589,000, while their "establishment survey" showed a reduction of payrolls of only 190,000. This shows that most of the damage is being done in small business, "under the radar screen" of the BLS.

Small businesses—especially *new* small businesses—account for essentially all net job growth. However, business creation and expansion requires capital, and more and more of the nation's capital is being commandeered by the U.S. Treasury in the name of "stimulus".

The FY [fiscal year] 2009 Federal deficit was $1.4 trillion. This was almost a trillion dollars higher than FY2008. The capital to buy this additional debt had to come from *somewhere*, and much of it was squeezed out of business. Here are some indicators, both statistical and anecdotal:

- During FY2009, "Gross Domestic Private Investment" fell by 25% (almost $500 billion/year). It would have needed to *grow* by 5% to keep the unemployment rate from rising from an already-too-high 6.2%.
- Many venture capital firms are informing entrepreneurs that there is no money available for new startups. The firms say that they must husband their capital to meet the needs of their existing portfolio companies.
- The 500 largest U.S. non-financial companies now hold more than $1 trillion in Treasury bills, amounting to more than 10% of their total assets. Corporate cash flows are rising, but the money is being invested in government bonds, rather than growth.
- Banks have cut credit card credit lines by 25%, or $1.25 trillion. Because small businesses are often financed with personal credit cards, this has a direct impact on small business survival and growth.

If you divide the total real capital employed in the U.S. ("produced assets") by total employment, you get about $313,000. That is, for $313,000 in capital, the private economy can create one real, permanent, self-supporting job. In contrast, there are estimates that each of the jobs that the administration claims that "stimulus" has "created or saved" is costing about $1.2 million.

If so, this means that selling the bonds required to fund one temporary "stimulus" job will take enough capital out of the private sector to destroy four "real" jobs. This explains why, as the "stimulus" spending has ramped up, job losses have accelerated.

No More Stimulus

Unfortunately, the [Barack Obama] Administration, the mainstream media, and much of the economics profession are responding to the worsening unemployment with calls for even more "stimulus". This would compound the tragedy. Each $313,000 of bonds sold to fund the additional spending could be expected to extinguish one private sector job. In addition, we can expect that the next increment of stimulus would be even more wasteful than the first $787 billion. The "best" projects would have been included in the first stimulus bill [the American Recovery and Reinvestment Act of 2009].

The "headline"(U-3) unemployment rate [the official unemployment measure] of 10.2% vastly understates the magnitude of the jobs crisis in America. John Williams' "Shadow Government Statistics" [a newsletter that challenges government economic statistics] unemployment number for October is 22.1%. Williams estimates that we would have to create 22.6 million new jobs in order to get to "true" full employment. At $313,000 each, the private sector would have to invest an incremental $7.1 trillion to accomplish this.

Every year for the past 58 years, real GDP has been very close to 30% of total capital employed (real "produced assets"). Accordingly, an additional $7.1 trillion in private business investment could be expected to increase GDP by about $2.1 trillion/year. Most of this income would go to the 22.6 million new job holders and their families, but about a quarter of it would be captured by governments at all levels.

Canceling the job-destroying "stimulus" program would be a good first step toward providing the private sector with the additional capital required to achieve full employment. However, this would provide only about 10% of the money required. The rest would have to be mobilized by increasing incentives for real savings and investment.

The two most effective measures toward this end would be to stabilize the dollar and to repeal the corporate income tax. The corporate income tax brought in only $138 billion in FY2009. This amounts to less than 1% of GDP, and less than a fifth of the cost of the "stimulus" bill. Repealing it now would produce higher employment and higher Federal revenues within months.

"Our green recovery program is an effective engine of job creation compared to spending the same amount of money within the oil industry or on household consumption."

Investing in Green Jobs Will Reduce Unemployment

Robert Pollin et al.

In the following viewpoint, economics professor Robert Pollin and his associates claim that government investment in environmentally friendly, "green," industries would result in job growth for the United States. Pollin explains that green investments—such as alternative energy, home retrofitting for energy efficiency, and expanding public transportation systems—would create millions of new employment opportunities and help decarbonize the economy. Pollin asserts that investing in the oil industry or buttressing public consumption would not provide the same employment benefits as a government-backed green growth strategy. Robert Pollin and his colleagues are members of the Political Economy Research Institute at the University of Massachusetts, Amherst.

Robert Pollin et al., *Green Recovery: A Program to Create Good Jobs and Start Building a Low-Carbon Economy*. Washington, DC: Center for American Progress, September 2008.

As you read, consider the following questions:

1. About how long would it take for investments in smart grids to create jobs and new spending, according to Pollin?
2. How many "direct jobs" do Pollin and his associates predict will be created if the government invested $100 billion in the six green investment areas?
3. What are the three factors that would help green investment programs create more jobs than investing in oil or public spending, in Pollin's view?

New job activities would certainly be created by building a green economy. Some of these jobs will be in specialized areas, such as installing solar panels and researching new building material technologies. But the vast majority of jobs are in the same areas of employment that people already work in today, in every region and state of the country.

Constructing wind farms, for example, creates jobs for sheet metal workers, machinists, and truck drivers, among many others. Increasing the energy efficiency of buildings through retrofitting requires roofers, insulators, and building inspectors. Expanding mass transit systems employs civil engineers, electricians, and dispatchers. More generally, this green economic recovery program will provide a major boost to the construction and manufacturing sectors throughout the United States through much-needed spending on green infrastructure.

In addition, all of these green energy investment strategies engage a normal range of service and support activities—including accountants, lawyers, office clerks, human resource managers, cashiers, and retail sales people. . . .

While all six of our investment areas[1] are crucial to accomplishing the long-term goal of rebuilding the U.S. economy on a low-carbon foundation, it doesn't follow that they all can contribute equally to a short-term green economic recovery program. Some of our investment strategies are clearly capable of delivering within a year, while others will require as long as two years to be implemented.

Retrofitting Buildings

The most obvious option for rapid green investment in communities is a large-scale building retrofit program, which would rely entirely on known technologies such as high-performance windows, efficient heating, ventilation and air conditioning systems, geothermal heating and cooling systems, efficient lighting and day-lighting, building-integrated photovoltaic-powered energy, and the installation of efficient appliances. Retrofitting can begin almost immediately on buildings of all sizes, in all regions of the country, and can provide short-term returns on the money being invested. Existing federal programs that could serve as vehicles for this swift investment include but are not limited to:

- Fully funding weatherization assistance to the level authorized by the Energy Independence and Security Act
- Expanding the energy-efficiency retrofit program in the Low Income Home Energy Assistance Program
- Matching state public benefit funds and other locally based programs supporting energy efficiency and green building retrofits to both public and private buildings.

To achieve the most rapid and effective short-term economic recovery program through a program of building retrofits, the U.S. government should require the retrofitting of

1. Retrofitting buildings, expanding mass transit and freight rail, constructing smart energy grids, and expanding production of wind power, solar power, and next-generation biofuels.

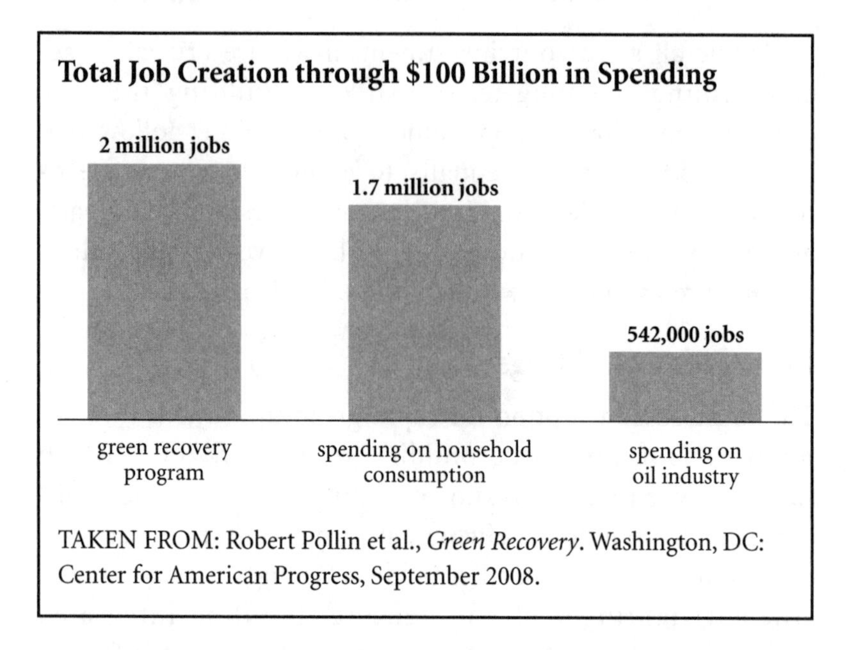

TAKEN FROM: Robert Pollin et al., *Green Recovery*. Washington, DC: Center for American Progress, September 2008.

all public buildings, which could commence as soon as Congress appropriated the funds, and should include measures to ensure state and local government participation as well. . . .

Mass Transit and Freight Rail

Public investment in expanding mass transit systems and freight rail networks in the United States could begin immediately in some areas but would take longer in others. In the mass transit arena, investments that could be pursued in very short order include, but are not limited to:

- Expanded bus and subway services
- Lower public transportation fares
- Expanded federal support for state and municipal transit operation and maintenance budgets to deal with increased ridership
- Increased federal subsidies for employer-based mass transit incentives

- Higher funding for critical mass transit programs currently bottlenecked for lack of federal dollars to encourage new ridership and more transportation choices.

Other areas, such as building light-rail or subway systems, will entail long lead times before a large amount of new hiring and spending occurs, but higher funding for existing mass transit and light rail projects would result in job growth in engineering, electrical work, welding, metal fabrication, and engine assembly sectors. Investing in diverse transportation options is important in both urban and rural communities, and can be an engine for far broader economic activity.

Upgrades to our freight rail through public investment would also yield some immediate job gains in similar professions, creating substantial employment through both construction and operations, alongside a down payment on more job creation over two years through improved maintenance and expansion of services. Existing federal programs through which these investments could be made quickly include expanding federal support and underwriting for freight rail infrastructure and rural economic development programs.

Smart Grids

Some smart grid investment projects are already in planning stages around the country. The projects entail combining advances in information technology with innovations in power system management to create a significantly more efficient distribution system for electrical energy. Through a green economic recovery program the U.S. government could deploy swift federal government support for these pilot projects.

Most smart grid investment initiatives, however, would require at least one year before significant levels of new spending and hiring could occur. Still, over the course of two years, new job opportunities with significant income growth potential could flourish; especially in locations where state utility policy is also designed to promote the efficiency of generation and distribution of electricity, through policies such as decoupling electricity sales from profits. . . .

Renewable Energy

In our three renewable energy areas—wind, solar, and next-generation biofuels—public- and private-sector investment growth is already picking up pace, with renewable energy technology supporting sustained double-digit rates of growth nationwide. Yet an unstable policy environment and the lack of long-term incentives have hurt the investment climate for these technologies, preventing them from realizing even greater growth. With sufficiently generous and stable federal tax incentives and credit subsidies, significant new private-sector investment would flow naturally and quickly into these three renewable energy arenas.

Existing federal programs through which these new green economic recovery funds could flow include renewing and expanding the investment tax credit and production tax credit for solar and wind energy. In addition, federal policy can be instrumental in building the infrastructure for next-generation biofuels, and federal loan guarantees are critical for moving rapidly to the next generation of advanced biofuels, where new companies face significant financing hurdles to break ground on next-generation manufacturing facilities that operate at a commercial scale. . . .

How a Green Recovery Program Creates Jobs

There are many ways government spending as a part of an economic recovery program can create jobs. Public spending directed toward a green recovery program, however, would result in more jobs than spending in many other areas, including, for example, within the oil industry or on increasing household consumption, which was the primary aim of the April 2008 stimulus program.

There, are three sources of job creation associated with any expansion of spending—direct, indirect, and induced effects. For purposes of illustration, consider these categories in terms of investments in home retrofitting or building wind turbines:

- *Direct effects.* Construction jobs created by retrofitting buildings to make them more energy efficient, or manufacturing jobs created to build wind turbines;
- *Indirect effects.* Manufacturing and service jobs created in associated industries that supply intermediate goods for building retrofits or wind turbine manufacturing, such as lumber, steel, and transportation;
- *Induced effects.* Retail and wholesale jobs created by workers in these construction, manufacturing, and service industries when they spend the money they earn on other products in the economy. . . .

From spending $100 billion in public funds in a combination of our six green investment areas, we estimate the number [of jobs created] at about 935,000 million direct jobs, 586,000 indirect jobs, and 496,000 induced jobs, for a total of about 2 million total jobs created. . . .

Other Benefits of Green Investment

Our green recovery program is an effective engine of job creation compared to spending the same amount of money within the oil industry or on household consumption. Increasing spending by $100 billion on household consumption along the lines of the April 2008 stimulus program would create about 1.7 million total jobs, or about 16 percent fewer jobs than the green recovery program. In addition to creating more jobs with a green investment program rather than increasing household consumption, targeting an economic stimulus program at increasing green investments also offers longer-term benefits: consumer savings by reducing home energy bills; stabilizing the price of oil, natural gas, and other non-renewable energy sources through reduced demand and increased energy diversity; and, of course, building over time a low-carbon economy.

Spending $100 billion within the domestic oil industry would create only about 542,000 jobs in the United States. A green infrastructure investment program would create nearly four times more jobs than spending the same amount of money on oil energy resources. And again, spending on oil offers no benefits in transitioning the U.S. economy toward a low-carbon future, while perpetuating the economic and national security vulnerabilities by continuing to rely on oil for the lifeblood of our economy.

Why does the green investment program create more jobs than spending within the oil industry or on household consumption? Three factors are at work.

Relative Labor Intensity

Relative to spending within the oil industry, the green investment program utilizes far more of its overall $100 billion in spending on hiring people, and less on purchasing machines and supplies. These direct and indirect effects on job creation are the primary explanation why the green investment program creates nearly four times more jobs than spending on oil. . . .

Domestic Content

The green investment program relies much more on products and services made within the U.S. economy and less on imports compared to spending either within the oil industry or on household consumption. These direct and indirect effects on job creation are the most significant reason why the green investment stimulus program creates more jobs than a household consumption stimulus. . . .

Pay Levels

Green investments generate not only significant numbers of well-paying jobs with benefits but also a relatively high proportion of lower, entry-level jobs that offer career ladders that can move low-paid workers into better employment positions over time. . . .

A green infrastructure investment program creates more jobs at all wage levels than spending within the oil industry because of both higher labor intensity and greater domestic content—resulting in average wages that are lower than the oil industry but spread across a greater number of jobs created. This attribute is significant.

The average pay of the green investment program is about 14 percent higher than that for the industries associated with household consumption. So in comparison with an economic stimulus centered on expanding household consumption, the green recovery program creates more jobs total, more spending within the U.S. economy, and better paying jobs on average over time. This is in addition to the longer-term benefits in terms of building a clean energy economy and creating downward pressure on the price of oil.

"If the alternative-energy sector were really economically more efficient than other forms of energy, it would create all the wonderful jobs all by itself, without the assistance of Uncle Sam."

Investing in Green Jobs Will Not Reduce Unemployment

Kevin Hassett

In the following viewpoint, Kevin Hassett claims that government funding of green jobs is wrongheaded. In his opinion, any viable enterprise should be able to create employment opportunities based on its desirability and performance. Hassett argues that green technologies have neither of these. He states that because alternative energies and other environmental industries are not stable enough to compete in the marketplace, artificially funding jobs in those fields is a risky and fiscally irresponsible move. Hassett maintains that other market-friendly alternatives would achieve green objectives with less disruption and cost. Hassett is the director of economic policy studies at the American Enterprise Institute for Public Policy Research, an organization dedicated to preserving free enterprise in the United States.

Kevin Hassett, "Hand over Your Job If You Want to Dream in Green," Bloomberg.com, October 5, 2009.

As you read, consider the following questions:

1. According to the author, what are the two future outcomes that economist J.D. Foster foresees if America was faced with his "rickshaw" plan to improve the environment?
2. According to Hassett, how many American dollars did Spain's green employment program spend for each job it artificially created?
3. What does Hassett believe is the best way to move the economy toward a cleaner future?

There may be nothing so dangerous as a policy fantasy. A good one is like the H1N1 [flu] virus. It spreads on contact and threatens to infect everyone in its path.

Policy fantasies are dangerous because they cause direct harm, replacing plans that might actually work, and because they spread economic illiteracy that can negatively influence future policies. If we want to address global warming, and we should, we need to adopt a carbon tax or cap-and-trade program to penalize greenhouse-gas emissions. Just about anything else is a distraction.

Right now [October 2009], one of the most dangerous policy fantasies is the distracting notion that government can create so-called green jobs and should strive to do so enthusiastically.

While the principal proponent of the green jobs hokum, [former Special Advisor for Green Jobs] Van Jones, is now out of government, the idea still influences policy design. Witness the Renew Through Green Jobs Act of 2009, which is making its way through Congress. President Barack Obama, of course, has been a veritable Typhoid Mary [disease carrier] of the green job virus, promising to deliver 5 million of them.

The analysis to back that up, and spread by green job enthusiasts such as Jones and many of his colleagues at the Center for American Progress, is that transferring society's resources to the green sector leads to a net creation of jobs. And it provides a tasty free lunch by cleaning the environment.

The Cost of Transfering Resources from One Sector to Another

Economics teaches, of course, that there are no free lunches. A key force driving such calculations is that alternative-energy production or energy conservation are fairly labor intensive relative to, say, the oil industry. But if the alternative-energy sector were really economically more efficient than other forms of energy, it would create all the wonderful jobs all by itself, without the assistance of Uncle Sam.

If, even after all the subsidies that government already provides to green technologies, we have to also subsidize training for workers in that industry, that suggests we are throwing money at an industry that can't pass the market test.

The notion is that we make ourselves better off by transferring resources from one sector, which is fairly efficient, to another, which isn't. Such an assertion might be correct if we account for the damage done by greenhouse gases. But with regard to job creation, the argument is nonsense.

Heritage Foundation economist J.D. Foster recently wrote that the same logic would recommend an even better and greener plan: the federal government could require that we all move about in rickshaws.

The logic is sound, is it not? It will take many environmentally friendly rickshaws to replace the passenger miles currently devoted to travel in cars and buses. With unemployment so high, a rickshaw program could reap huge economic benefits.

Or would it?

In the long run, when real wages and workers have the opportunity to adjust, the economy tends toward full employment. One simply can't redistribute resources and change the number of jobs. So we get to choose in the long run between an economy with lots of rickshaws and an economy with more efficient transportation, and lots of jobs in other sectors.

In the short run, when unemployment is high, then the government can conceivably create jobs. If it does so by transferring resources from one sector to another, then one must be careful to net the jobs lost in one sector against the jobs gained in another.

Spain Provides a Cautionary Lesson

Even if we use deficit spending and borrow money from the Chinese to create jobs, we can't be sure that the net creation is very large. If consumers understand correctly that the big deficit means higher future taxes, they will cut their consumption, and businesses outside the green industry will reduce production and employment.

Obama has consistently used Spain as an example of green job paradise.

Spain has, indeed, invested heavily in green jobs. And the results? A recent study by Spanish economist Gabriel Calzada Alvarez and colleagues at the Universidad Rey Juan Carlos, found that the Spanish program spent 571,138 euros for every job it created. That's about $833,000 per job.

The Spanish program also sucked resources out of more productive sectors into less productive ones, costing 2.2 jobs for every green job created.

Penalize Carbon Production

While Alvarez's calculations rely on assumptions that might overstate the case a bit, consider the impact of the Obama green jobs program if his numbers are correct. The president has promised to create 5 million green jobs. If he succeeds, then it will cost 11 million jobs in other sectors, and the medium-term increase in unemployment will be 6 million jobs.

To put that in perspective, the number of unemployed Americans has increased in the past two years by 7.6 million. Creating 5 million green jobs would do almost the same amount of net harm.

Environmental programs should be weighed on their merits. The most efficient way to move toward a cleaner future is to provide incentives to rely on alternative energy with a penalty on carbon. If a carbon tax causes some unemployment, we can address that with tax reductions elsewhere. The green jobs fantasy makes the adoption of such a plan harder, and, to the extent that it affects real policy, hurts real people.

Periodical Bibliography

The following articles have been selected to supplement the diverse views presented in this chapter.

Peter Coy and Roger Runningen	"The Case for More Stimulus," *BusinessWeek*, April 19, 2010.
Economist	"Something's Not Working," May 1, 2010.
Emily Ethridge	"Help Wanted: New Plan for Unemployment," *CQ Weekly*, April 12, 2010.
William P. Hoar	"Stimulus Spawns More Debt and Government Jobs," *New American*, March 29, 2010.
Paul Krugman	"Punishing the Jobless," *New York Times*, July 5, 2010.
Wayne Lenell	"The 'HIRE' Act of 2010," *Priest*, July 2010.
Sarah Lozanova	"Defining Green Jobs," *Planning*, April 2010.
John Maggs	"Where Are the Jobs?" *National Journal*, June 12, 2010.
Iain Murray	"Green Jobs and Rose-Tinted Glasses," *National Review*, March 8, 2010.
Sara Murray	"Long Recession Ignites Debate on Jobless Benefits," *Wall Street Journal*, July 7, 2010.
New Republic	"Austerity Nuts," July 8, 2010.
Robert Pollin	"18 Million Jobs by 2012," *Nation*, March 8, 2010.
Hilda Solis and Diana Furchtgott-Roth	"Are 'Green' Jobs an Important Potential Source of New Jobs?" *CQ Researcher*, June 4, 2010.

What Can Policy Makers and Businesses Do to Reduce Unemployment?

Chapter Preface

"With the national unemployment rate rising rapidly, a key question facing state and federal governments is how best to help workers who have lost their jobs. One-Stop Career Centers (One-Stops), first established in the 1980s, may prove critical in this effort." So begins the Brookings Institution's Hamilton Project Policy Brief of April 2009, titled "Strengthening One-Stop Career Centers: Helping More Unemployed Workers Find Jobs and Build Skills." In the brief, Louis S. Jacobson of CNA, an economic think tank, claims that One-Stop Career Centers serve around 15 million job seekers each year and provide them with job search assistance and training programs, some of which are covered by unemployment insurance benefits. Jacobson reports that these institutions, which have been in service for nearly three decades, have recently had their budgets slashed as federal funding has dropped from $1.4 billion (adjusted for inflation) in 1990 to about 700 million today. Jacobson bemoans these cuts because, in his view, the services that One-Stop Career Centers provide are very cost effective and can be tailored to become even more fiscally responsible.

Although Jacobson admits some One-Stops have wasted federal funds on services that do not match or sometimes exceed client's needs, he believes that greater accountability can ensure that these expenditures end. For example, Jacobson writes that "One-Stops already collect data on clients receiving intensive services and could use these data to measure returns to training." In his opinion, this would allow policy makers to "create performance measures that direct resources toward services proven to be the most cost effective." Jacobson contends that with more funding, better-regulated One-Stops could provide more core services (such as job searching) to a greater number of unemployed clients while reserving intensive services (such as counseling and training) for select clients who have a proven need for them and a proven desire to continue their job hunt. He believes that with a new $4 billion government investment over two years, One-Stop Career Centers could help an additional 5.6 million workers each year.

Finding $4 billion dollars in the federal budget remains difficult in such lean times, but Jacobson claims the return on investment would be substantial—especially if the goal is getting Americans back to work. Arguing that unemployed people who find work more quickly will use fewer unemployment benefits and generate more tax money, Jacobson states the "total benefits to society, which include benefits to both workers and taxpayers, would amount to $7.7 billion per year."

The authors in the following chapter offer other possible solutions to cut the national unemployment rate. Each of these solutions has a cost to society—mainly in terms of tax dollars or lost wages—that makes many people hesitant to agree to the implementation of the strategies. However, given the weak public-sector job creation in the years following the 2008 financial crisis, policy makers may have to choose more radical remedies to reemploy America.

"There are a few things the government can do about persistent long-term unemployment."

Government Job Creation and Job Security Programs Will Lessen Unemployment

Daniel Gross

In the following viewpoint, Daniel Gross argues that there are a few steps the government can take to lower the unemployment rate. In Gross's opinion, the safety net of unemployment insurance and benefits can be expanded so that the unemployed can stay current on bills, rent, and mortgage. Secondly, the author believes that enacting policies that create and preserve jobs—such as public work programs, summer job programs, and tax cuts—will reduce long-term unemployment. Daniel Gross writes a twice-weekly column for Slate *magazine and is a senior editor at* Newsweek *magazine.*

As you read, consider the following questions:

1. In Gross's opinion, why hasn't the government enacted any policies or taken any steps toward combating persistent long-term unemployment?

Daniel Gross, "Does Anyone Care About Unemployment Anymore?" *Newsweek*, July 1, 2010. Reproduced by permission.

2. According to Nevada Senate candidate Sharron Angle's opinion, what is responsible for her state's unemployment rate?
3. As stated by Gross in the viewpoint, what seems to be Obama's plan regarding the stimulus?

Today's new Labor Department report showing that the economy lost jobs last month [June 2010], the first loss this year, seems in stark contrast to where the president and the Congress are focusing their attentions. Congress is adjourning without extending unemployment benefits, in large measure due to repeated Republican filibusters [the right to unlimited congressional debate]. And on Thursday [July 1, 2010], President [Barack] Obama gave a major address about . . . immigration reform.

The economy is now presenting a strange dichotomy. The corporate sector has returned to rude health, with improved balance sheets and tons of cash. It has helped lead the recovery. But without the mighty American consumer, who generates 70 percent of economic activity, participating to the fullest degree, the recovery will seem anemic. Without a healthy jobs market, the recession-shocked consumer won't spend.

What the Government Can Do About Unemployment

And yet Washington's response seems to be a collective throwing up of hands. There are a few things the government can do about persistent long-term unemployment. First, it can lessen the pain it causes by expanding the safety net, extending unemployment-insurance benefits so that the long-term unemployed have a source of cash to help them stay current on rent, mortgage, and credit card bills. Second, it can respond to persistent long-term unemployment by enacting policies aimed at creating and preserving jobs. These can take the form of summer jobs programs, enhanced public works programs, aid to strapped municipalities so they can avoid layoffs, and tax cuts and credits for investment and hiring.

But so far? Nothing. And the question is why.

First, there's the matter of the uncertain trumpet at the Fed [Federal Reserve]. When I wrote last week that Federal Reserve Chairman Ben Bernanke didn't seem particularly bummed about high unemployment, a reader asked what I expected him to do. At the very least, he could have lent moral support to the need for further stimulus—if only out of self-interest. Maybe he wants to be remembered as the Fed chairman who presided over an era of European-level unemployment, when skills eroded, and several graduating classes entered a glutted workforce.

But the two branches of government responsible for initiating and implementing fiscal policy haven't acted with a sense of urgency, either. And politics clearly has a lot to do with it. On the fringes of the Republican right, there's some flat-out Randian [referring to twentieth century novelist Ayn Rand] lunacy—i.e., Nevada Senate candidate Sharron Angle arguing that laziness and a desire to live large off unemployment checks is responsible for her state's 14 percent unemployment rate. There's some parochialism. Sen. Ben Nelson, a Democrat from Nebraska, a state where the unemployment rate is about half the national average, joined the Republican filibuster of an extension of unemployment benefits—his constituents don't need it. In the broad center, there's a lot of serious hypocritical deficit-hawk nonsense. Along with many other senators, Nelson opposed the recent benefit extension on the grounds that it was immoral and wrong to enact a $19 billion spending package without offsetting tax increases or spending cuts. Funny how such probity never surfaces when legislators vote to spend much larger sums on the wars in Iraq and Afghanistan, on the Medicare prescription drug benefit, and on the [George W.] Bush tax cuts. Meanwhile, on his Web site, Nelson regularly touts deficit-fueled stimulus spending being funneled to Nebraska.

We May Have to Accept High Levels of Unemployment

In the White House, there's probably a level of exhaustion and Zen-like acceptance—it pushed through a large stimulus package and monumental health care reform, two heroic measures that are working and whose benefits will continue to phase in over time. These efforts have exhausted the policy team and its congressional allies. And perhaps high unemployment is something we'll have to live with, given the way the economy has recovered from recent recessions. The president's budget notes "even with healthy economic growth there is likely to be an extended period of higher-than-normal unemployment lasting for several years." A chart in the budget notes that after the 1991 and 2002 recessions, the turning points for jobs came five and seven quarters, respectively, after the trough in growth. If there's a sense that all modern recoveries will be jobless, as companies focus on productivity and offshoring, then further stimulus provides diminishing economic and political returns.

This sort of political maneuvering is entirely predictable. My suspicion is that too many people in Washington think it's smart short-term politics not to demand urgent action on unemployment. Centrist Democrats and the White House seem to have decided that pushing too hard for more stimulus will leave them open to Republican charges that they're boosting the deficit. Besides, it's too late to do anything that will have an impact before October [2010], when voters make up their mind. They're probably right. Obama's plan seems to be to let the stimulus work, to triangulate between an angry left and an angry right, and hope and expect that the economy will be better in October 2012 than it is in October 2010. And he's probably right. Republicans have made the calculation that the weaker the economy and the employment market are in the next few months, the better their prospects for 2010 and 2012 are—and they're right, too.

But they're also wrong. Forget about the damage to the economy at large, or to those people who aren't working. For both parties, whether you're a deficit hawk, a tax-cutting obsessive, or an incumbent bent on re-election in 2010 or 2012—persistent high unemployment is poison. Payroll and income taxes—in other words, taxes paid by people with jobs—provide the lion's share of federal tax revenues. For Democrats, there's no way to cut the deficit or find revenue for new initiatives unless they grow. Should Republicans retake control of the House and Senate next year, their first order of business would be to preserve the Bush tax cuts that are set to expire—a move that would make already large deficits even larger and thus render significant tax-reduction impossible.

Viewpoint

"Our workforce includes 13.5 million people who don't belong in it at all."

Raising Taxes to Pay for Education and Increased Social Security Benefits Will Reduce Unemployment

Moshe Adler

Millions of jobs in America are filled by people near retirement age or by young people who need money for college. In the following viewpoint, Moshe Adler argues that by raising taxes an average of 11 percent, America could afford to pay for increased Social Security payments for older workers and for the tuition of all college-age individuals. By doing so, Adler expects that these young and old workers would be persuaded to leave the workforce, opening up their jobs to the nation's unemployed working-age adults. Adler contends that this solution would serve the well-being of individuals and benefit the country's flagging economy. Moshe Adler is a teacher of economics at Columbia University.

As you read, consider the following questions:

1. In Adler's view, how can the government compensate families for the loss of $19 billion in wages if high school students are culled from the workforce?
2. According to Adler's calculations, what would be the cost to American taxpayers if all college-age adults were given a free education?
3. Why does Adler claim that the number of "positions seeking workers" will increase if his plan is adopted?

Ten percent of Americans are unemployed, and many doubt that President [Barack] Obama's stimulus will create enough jobs to reduce this rate significantly. But given the structure of our labor force, more jobs is not necessarily what we need anyway. Our workforce includes 13.5 million people who don't belong in it at all. Permitting them not to work would free up jobs and raise the wages of millions of workers who belong in the middle class. It would also free all of us of our dependence on Wall Street.

Currently [as of October 2009], four million children under the age of eighteen work, filling the equivalent of two million full time jobs. (The actual number is higher. Even though the law permits the employment of children over the age of fourteen, the Census Bureau only collects data about workers who are older than sixteen.) Ten million college-age youth (between the ages of eighteen and twenty one) also work, and they fill the equivalent of eight million full time jobs. Five million of these college-age youth do not attend college at all. Finally, there are also four and a half million workers who are sixty six years or older, and they fill the equivalent of three and a half million full time jobs. The questions before us are then: Should these workers be removed from the workforce? How much would this cost? Can we afford it? And finally, what will our lives look like after all these workers stop working?

Subsidizing Education to Keep Kids out of the Workplace

That high school students don't belong in the workforce does not require an explanation. Of course, the families of these children need the money they earn, but their earnings are very small, just $19 billion in 2007, and they could be replaced by child subsidies to low income families.

That high school grads belong in college is also pretty obvious. Today, workers must have a college education in order to do well. In 1950 the difference between the wage of a college graduate and a high school graduate was 27%. But by 2000 this gap grew to 75%. Nevertheless, just as the importance of having a college education has been increasing, it has become dramatically less affordable. Between 1981 and 2005 tuition in state universities increased four times faster than personal incomes did. Making college education free would both increase the number of youth who go to college and decrease the need of those who are already in college to work.

Of course, providing all interested high school graduates with a free college education plus stipends cost will not be cheap. The average yearly tuition in public colleges is currently $6,585 and this figure covers 40% of the total cost of education. If all young adults chose to go to college, and assuming that tuition was entirely free, the additional cost to taxpayers would be $164 billion a year. The salaries and wages that all college age workers earned, both students and non-students, in 2007, was $135 billion. If the lost earnings are fully replaced by student-stipends, the total cost of providing college education to all would be some $300 billion.

That old people ought to be able to retire shouldn't be controversial. But the social security payment of the median retiree amounts to just forty-two percent of the income she earned while working, and it is not surprising that many workers are forced to continue working even when they are old. Doubling retiree benefits would cost an additional $505 billion a year, and it is the most expensive item in our proposal.

Paying for the Plan

No doubt, not all young adults who are offered the opportunity to go to college will take advantage of it, and not all older Americans will retire even with higher social security payments. But for argument's sake if we assume that all these individuals will in fact leave, the cost of removing thirteen and a half million workers from the workforce, and giving all young adults free college education would come to $825 billion a year. This may sound like a large sum, but it is actually just 11% of the total income that households earn, excluding the wages and salaries of the workers who will no longer work.

Can we afford an average increase of 11% in taxes (a higher increase for the rich, smaller increase for the poor)? Let's recall that between 1913, the year in which the income tax became constitutional, and 1981, the first year of the [Ronald] Reagan presidency, the highest marginal tax rate was on average 68%. Today it is 35%.

A More Stable and Equitable Future for All

What will our lives be like if millions of low-wage workers stop working? The most visible effect will probably be a drastic reduction in the number of stores that are open 24 hours a day, because it is the abundance of workers that keeps these stores open in the wee hours of the night, when there is nary a customer.

But the most significant change will come from the shift to government financed higher education and retirement. Our lives will be remarkably more secure when we will no longer have to entrust our fate and the fate of our children to retirement and college savings invested in stocks. And when this happens, the incomes and the political power of stock brokers will decline precipitously; Main Street will no longer be in the clutches of Wall Street.

Inequality would decline dramatically as well. With five million fewer retail and restaurant workers, a million fewer construction and a million fewer manufacturing workers, and a six million reduction in the numbers of workers available for work in all other industries, wages will rise significantly. Furthermore, the number of positions seeking workers will increase too, because in order to accommodate five million additional students, the number of jobs on colleges will have to increase by three and a half million. And if millions of old workers will be able to retire, the services that cater to them will also have to increase.

The current crisis inflicts great harm on middle class and low-wage workers. But what we don't want is to return to the world as it was before the crisis. That world deprived millions of children of childhood and the chance for a good education; it prevented millions of youth from being able to attend college; and it deprived millions of old people from being able to retire. It also made all of us dependent on Wall Street. Instead, let's make sure that families have enough money to support their children, that high school grads can afford to go to college, and that older workers who want to retire can.

> *"According to the Census Bureau, 1 out of every 6 workers is foreign born."*

Lowering Immigration Will Reduce Unemployment

Virgil Goode

In the viewpoint that follows, Virgil Goode argues that the number of immigrants to the United States has risen in recent decades, increasing the competition for domestic jobs. In today's poor economy, such unrestricted immigration ultimately results in fewer jobs for native-born Americans, Goode claims. He believes many politicians are unfortunately endorsing this open-door policy when they should be calling for a moratorium on immigration to free up jobs for Americans. Virgil Goode represented Virginia in the U.S. House of Representatives from 1997 to 2009.

As you read, consider the following questions:

1. According to statistics that Goode quoted from the Department of Homeland Security, how many permanent green cards did the U.S. government issue to working-age immigrants in 2009?

Virgil Goode, "Unemployment and the Immigration Glut," *FrontPage Magazine*, May 28, 2010.

2. What percentage of immigrants come from Europe, according to Goode, and why does Goode cite this statistic?
3. As Goode states, who is the principle sponsor of the SAFE (Security and Fairness Enhancement) for America Act, and what does this act propose to do?

With 10% unemployment [in May 2010], one would think that the government would consider lowering the number of green cards issued to foreign workers until Americans were back on their feet. Amazingly, recently released data from the Department of Homeland Security shows that we have actually increased immigration. Far from reflecting supply and demand, our legal immigration numbers continue to climb no matter the state of the national economy.

The latest figures come from fiscal year 2009. The fiscal year began on October 1, 2008, which is when our economic collapse began and continued through September of 2009. Over five million Americans lost their jobs over that period.

Foreign-Born Workers Swarm America

America issued 1,130,818 permanent green cards, 808,478 of which were given to immigrants of working age. This is an increase over 2008 and 2007. Excluding the extra green cards given after the 1986 amnesty, this was the second highest number of green cards issued since 1914. From 2000 through 2009, we issued 10,299,430—the highest decade in American history.

In addition to the green cards, the government issued 881,840 temporary work visas and gave refugee or asylum status to 96,721 aliens. The total increase to the American workforce was 1.75 million foreign workers. According to the Census Bureau, 1 out of every 6 workers is foreign born.

What are the possible justifications for this policy? Are these immigrants taking jobs Americans won't do? With the unemployment rate at nearly 10%, no one can say this with a straight face.

Does this create diversity? The pool of legal immigrants is rather un-diverse. Less than 10% of them come from Europe.

Does this decrease illegal immigration? If that were the case, you would have expected the illegal immigration numbers to decline as legal immigration increased. In fact, they have both skyrocketed.

Politicians Abetting the Immigrant Glut

Instead of talking about reducing these numbers, politicians are calling for raising the level of legal immigration. Senators Chuck Schumer (D-NY), Robert Menendez (D-NJ), and Harry Reid (D-NV) recently released an outline for their ideas for "comprehensive immigration reform." They call for adding an additional 3.4 million family visas and 550,000 work visas.

In the House [of Representatives], Luis Gutierrez (D-IL) and Solomon Ortiz (D-TX) introduced the Comprehensive Immigration Reform for America's Security and Prosperity Act which makes the same proposals for increasing family and work visas, but one ups them by adding a special new visa category of 100,000 permanent green cards a year to go specifically to Latin American countries.

[In mid-2010] there are two bills in Congress that will reduce legal immigration. Rep. Phil Gingrey's (R-GA) Nuclear Family Priority Act will limit family based immigration and reduce 111,800 green cards. Rep. Bob Goodlatte's (R-VA) SAFE [Security and Fairness Enhancement] for America Act will eliminate the Visa Lottery category that grants 50,000 visas a year. Unfortunately, the Republican leadership is not backing these bills and they only have 30 and 57 co-sponsors, respectively.

These bills are a great start, but even if they passed we'd still issue nearly one million green cards a year. If we really want to put Americans back to work, we need a moratorium across nearly all categories of legal immigration. A moratorium will free up jobs for American citizens, reduce the stress on social services, and allow the immigrants already here to assimilate.

The only people who will lose out from a moratorium are the ethnic interests who want new constituents and the business lobbies who want cheap labor. Unfortunately, both political parties are more concerned with the well-being of these special interests than the well-being of American citizens.

VIEWPOINT 4

> *"The idea that foreign-born workers are stealing American jobs should be turned back at the border."*

Immigrants Are Not Responsible for High Unemployment

Viveca Novak

Viveca Novak is a member of FactCheck.Org, a project of the Annenberg Public Policy Center of the University of Pennsylvania. Novak has worked for the National Journal, *the* Wall Street Journal, *and* Time *magazine. In the following viewpoint, Viveca Novak refutes popular assertions that a flood of immigrants is responsible for high unemployment among native-born citizens in the United States. According to Novak, immigrants do not raise unemployment; instead, immigrants create jobs by consuming more goods and services. In addition, Novak claims immigrants—who usually enter the workforce at the bottom of the economic ladder—help increase wages for those already in the workforce by opening up more opportunities for managers, construction people, and other better-paying jobs that result from the expanding population of consumers.*

Viveca Novak, "Does Immigration Cost Jobs?" Factcheck.org, May 13, 2010.

As you read, consider the following questions:

1. As Novak reports, what organization was behind the ad that ran in Arizona in April 2010 and that drew a correlation between high unemployment and open immigration policies?
2. According to Novak, the wages of which native-born workers are adversely affected by immigrant populations?
3. According to one of President George W. Bush's economic reports, foreign-born workers comprised what percentage of the total workforce growth in the United States between 1996 and 2003?

Do immigrants take American jobs? It's a common refrain among those who want to tighten limits on legal immigration and deny a "path to citizenship"—which they call "amnesty"—to the millions of immigrants living in the U.S. illegally. There's even a new Reclaim American Jobs Caucus in the House [of Representatives], with at least 41 members.

But most economists and other experts say there's little to support the claim. Study after study has shown that immigrants grow the economy, expanding demand for goods and services that the foreign-born workers and their families consume, and thereby creating jobs. There is even broad agreement among economists that while immigrants may push down wages for some, the overall effect is to increase average wages for American-born workers.

Arizona's tough new law [passed in April 2010] targeting illegal immigrants and the possibility of congressional action on immigration have brought a renewed focus to the issue. Among lawmakers and others who seek stricter immigration limits and stronger enforcement, we've noticed a common theme that may have particular resonance at a time when the unemployment rate remains stuck at close to 10 percent: that immigrants take American jobs. But most who have studied the topic say it's not true. We'll explain after we show you some of the arguments being made.

Blaming Unemployment on Immigration

Exhibit A is an ad that ran in late April [2010] in Arizona. It was sponsored by the Coalition for the Future American Worker [CFAW], an organization that includes such groups as NumbersUSA and the Federation for American Immigration Reform, both of which seek to limit the number of people coming to the U.S. to live, legally or illegally. The spot's narrator, lamenting the high number of unemployed Americans, says that "with millions jobless, our government is still bringing in a million-and-a-half foreign workers a year to take American jobs."

Then there's the new group in the House of Representatives, the Reclaim American Jobs Caucus, which has at least 41 members. Republican Reps. Lamar Smith of Texas, Sue Myrick of North Carolina, and Gary Miller of California announced its formation in a video in March [2010], with Myrick saying: "Right now, with unemployment hovering around 10 percent, we thought it was time to talk about the direct link between unemployment and illegal immigration."

Miller makes it all sound so easy: Eight million illegal immigrants working in the U.S., 15 million unemployed American citizens and legal immigrants—we could cut the number of unemployed in half if we just booted out the illegal workers. "The numbers are simple," he says.

The numbers certainly *would* be simple, if they worked that way. But they don't.

Exhibit C is from GOP [Republican] Sen. Jim DeMint of South Carolina, a leader in the tea party movement [political movement, begun in 2009, that protests government waste and excessive government spending]. DeMint supports the new Arizona law, as do many tea partiers, and advocates its spread:

> *DeMint, May 6* [2010]: Every state will handle it differently. . . . South Carolina has already passed laws to crack down on illegal immigrants. Many other states are also under a lot of pressure because of high unemployment to not let illegal immigrants come and take jobs.

Immigrants Create Jobs

Exhibit A above, the CFAW ad, focuses on *legal* immigrants, those who have employment authorization documents or who are lawful permanent residents (often known as green card holders). According to a fact sheet posted by NumbersUSA to support the ad, the 1.5 million immigrants mentioned by the narrator is a combination of the two groups using 2007 figures. (The coalition had to do some double-counting to get to that figure, but delving into the math would take us off-topic.)

The video from the congressional caucus and the statement from Sen. DeMint refer specifically to *illegal* immigrants. According to the [research organization] Pew Hispanic Center, there were nearly 12 million undocumented immigrants in the U.S. in 2008, with 8.3 million in the labor force. About 5.4 percent of the nation's workforce, then, was composed of illegal immigrants.

But whether they're legal, as in the CFAW ad, or illegal, as in our two other examples, really doesn't matter for the purpose of answering our question: The truth is that immigrants don't "take American jobs," according to most economists and others who have studied the issue.

Immigrant workers "create almost as many" jobs as they occupy, "and maybe more," said Madeleine Sumption, policy analyst at the nonpartisan Migration Policy Institute, which is funded by a range of foundations, corporations and international organizations. "They often create the jobs they work in." In addition, "they buy things, and they make the economy bigger," she told us. As she and a co-author [Will Somerville] wrote in a report last year for a group created by the British government:

> *Somerville and Sumption*: [T]he impact of immigration [on a nation's economy] remains small, for several reasons. Immigrants are not competitive in many types of jobs, and hence are not direct substitutes for natives. Local employers increase demand for low-skilled labor in areas that receive low-skilled immigrant inflows. Immigrants contribute to demand for goods and services that they consume, in turn increasing the demand for labor. And immigrants contribute to labor market efficiency and long-term economic growth.

David Griswold, director of the Center for Trade Policy Studies at the libertarian Cato Institute, wrote in an article for *Commentary* magazine in December [2009]:

> *Griswold*: The addition of low-skilled immigrants expands the size of the overall economy, creating higher-wage openings for managers, craftsmen, accountants, and the like. The net result is a greater financial reward and relatively more opportunities for those Americans who finish high school.

And a new study by economist Heidi Shierholz of the Economic Policy Institute—a liberal think tank that has been funded in part by U.S. labor unions—says that:

> *Shierholz*: In the ongoing debate on immigration, there is broad agreement among academic economists that it has a small but positive impact on the wages of native-born workers overall: although new immigrant workers add to the labor supply, they also consume goods and services, which creates more jobs . . .

Lowering Some Wages, Raising Others

Both Griswold and Shierholz acknowledge that some workers may be harmed by an influx of immigrant labor. Griswold writes that "low-skilled immigrants do exert mild downward pressure on the wages of the lowest-paid American workers," though the overall impact on jobs and the economy is positive. Another economist, George Borjas, an advocate of clamping down on immigration, found that between 1980 and 2000 native-born Americans without a high school education saw their wages decline 7.4 percent because of immigrant labor.

Shierholz found that it's often other foreign-born workers—especially those who came to the U.S. several years earlier—who get the short end of the stick. But American workers benefit, she writes:

> *Shierholz*: A key result from this work is that the estimated effect of immigration from 1994 to 2007 was to raise the wages of U.S.-born workers, relative to foreign-born workers, by 0.4% (or $3.68 per week), and to lower the wages of foreign-born workers, relative to U.S.-born workers, by 4.6% (or $33.11 per week).

The consensus that immigrant workers expand the U.S. economy is broad, and crosses party lines. In 2005, the White House of Republican President George W. Bush remarked on the fact in one of its annual economic reports to Congress:

> *Economic Report of the President, Feb. 2005*: The foreign-born are associated with much of the employment growth in recent years. Between 1996 and 2003, when total employment grew by 11 million, 58 percent of the net increase was among foreign-born workers. . . . [E]mployment of natives as operators, fabricators, and laborers fell by 1.4 million between 1996 and 2002, while employment in such occupations grew by 930,000 among the foreign-born. This should not be taken as evidence that the foreign-born displace native workers; rather, it reflects the fact that immigrants have made up all of the growth in the low-skilled workforce.

The people [laid-off workers] pictured in the elevator in CFAW's ad aren't likely to be competing with immigrant labor for positions. There may be other reasons for an overhaul of current immigration policy. But the idea that foreign-born workers are stealing American jobs should be turned back at the border.

Periodical Bibliography

The following articles have been selected to supplement the diverse views presented in this chapter.

Jennifer Burnett	"High Unemployment Puts State Jobless Funds in the Red," *Capitol Ideas*, March/April 2010.
Tim Cavanaugh	"Five Lies About the American Economy," *Reason*, April 2010.
Paul Davidson	"Crafting Strategies to Create Jobs," *USA Today*, December 9, 2009.
Thomas L. Friedman	"Start-Ups, Not Bailouts," *New York Times*, April 4, 2010.
Brian Friel	"The Hard Work of Moving a Jobs Bill," *National Journal*, May 22, 2010.
Teresa Ghilarducci	"Employment Benefits," *America*, May 3, 2010.
Barbara Kiviat	"How to Create a Job," *Time*, March 29, 2010.
Lawrence Kudlow	"Tax Cuts Would End Jobs Crisis," *Human Events*, October 19, 2009.
Justin Lahart and Emmiline Zhao	"What Would You Do with an Extra Hour?" *Wall Street Journal*, June 23, 2010.
Nation	"Job Number 1—Jobs," June 28, 2010.
Motoko Rich	"A Jobless Rate Still Unaffected by New Hiring," *New York Times*, June 4, 2010.

For Further Discussion

Chapter 1

1. Given that many U.S. industries are outsourcing jobs to foreign nations with cheaper labor, many people blame globalization for high unemployment rates in the United States. Do you agree with these critics of globalization? Read the viewpoints by Darren Weeks, William H. Overholt, and Daniel Griswold, and cite which points you agree with (and why you agree with them) and what you would do to keep America competitive in a globalizing world while concurrently easing unemployment.
2. Martin Ford foresees a future in which unemployment will be rampant because human workers will no longer be needed to do the jobs robots and other artificial intelligence machines can do. Using the arguments from Jeff Burnstein and any other sources you can find, take the opposing view and point out the ways in which Ford's prediction might not be correct.
3. The debate over the usefulness of minimum wage hikes focuses on issues of human rights and economic justice. Christopher Jaarda insists that increases in the minimum wage make it difficult for businesses to employ as many unskilled workers, thus increasing unemployment. Holly Sklar argues that raising the minimum wage will help the economy overall by giving lower-income workers more spending cash. How do both authors use historical precedent to inform and support their conclusions? Whose argument do you find more convincing?

Chapter 2

1. According to Joel Dreyfuss, what circumstances are responsible for high rates of black unemployment in the United States? According to the U.S. Congress' Joint Economic Committee, what circumstances are contributing to high levels of Hispanic joblessness? Examine both sets of reasons and see if any are comparable. Then, explain why you think blacks and Hispanics might be sharing these similar economic woes.
2. Reread the viewpoints by Catherine Rampell and Emily Brandon and then list the reasons both young and older workers are supposedly being shut out of the job market. According to Rampell and Brandon, what alternatives are these job exiles pursuing? What positive and negative effects do you believe will result from so many people staying out of the job market?
3. Don Peck predicts that the increasing jobless rate among young people will negatively impact those individuals as well as American society at large. Choose three of Peck's predictions and explain whether you agree or disagree with his evidence or conclusions. You may use other viewpoints from this book and any outside readings to support your claims.

Chapter 3

1. The Congressional Budget Office (CBO) and Louis Woodhill claim that the purpose of the economic stimulus package was to provide businesses with money to increase job growth. After rereading the viewpoints, explain why Woodhill believes the stimulus money unfortunately ended up increasing unemployment. Do you think his assessment could be accurate? What evidence does he give that seems convincing? What evidence does the CBO give to persuade you otherwise?

2. Robert Pollin and his colleagues assert that investing in alternative energies and other "green" industries is both timely and prudent because it will reduce reliance on dwindling supplies of carbon fuels and build a new infrastructure that will need new workers. On the other hand, Kevin Hassett contends that spending money on alternative energies is unwise and will not lead to sustainable job growth. Explain why these authors are so diametrically opposed in their views. Then, explain which argument you find more plausible and why.

Chapter 4

1. Moshe Adler proposes a plan to increase taxes to pay for larger Social Security benefits for older Americans and free college tuition for young, would-be workers. He insists that this scheme would encourage millions of Americans that fall into these two categories to either retire or go to school, thus decreasing competition for employment among those left in the job market. Do you think Adler's plan could work? What advantages and flaws do you see? Explain.
2. Former U.S. Representative Virgil Goode claims that America's open-door immigration policy is harming the job prospects of native-born citizens. In his opinion, low-skilled immigrants are filling positions that should be reserved for Americans in times of economic crisis. Viveca Novak takes the opposing view, asserting that immigrants create more jobs by utilizing more services that consequently need more workers to handle the increasing number of consumers. Decide what kind of immigration policy you would impose on the United States and explain what impact you think your policy would have on unemployment. You may use arguments from the viewpoints to support your claims.

Organizations to Contact

The editors have compiled the following list of organizations concerned with the issues debated in this book. The descriptions are derived from materials provided by the organizations. All have publications or information available for interested readers. The list was compiled on the date of publication of the present volume; the information provided here may change. Be aware that many organizations take several weeks or longer to respond to inquiries, so allow as much time as possible.

American Enterprise Institute for Public Policy Research (AEI)
1150 Seventeenth St. NW, Washington, DC 20036
(202) 862-5800 • fax: (202) 862-7177
website: www.aei.org

AEI, a nonpartisan public policy organization, investigates a variety of topics impacting the United States and the world, ranging from economics to health policy and foreign policy to national defense. AEI supports the free market economy and contends that free markets provide the best opportunity for economic growth and prosperity. AEI scholars have addressed the growing unemployment problem in publications and speeches such as "Business Volatility, Job Destruction, and Unemployment," "Unemployment Insurance: Considerations for Extending Benefits," and "Unemployment in Europe and the U.S." Further information about the current economic climate in the United States and unemployment can be found in the bi-monthly magazine of AEI, *The American*.

American Federation of Labor and Congress of Industrial Organizations (AFL-CIO)
815 16th St. NW, Washington, DC 20006
websites: www.aflcio.org, www.workingamerica.org

The AFL-CIO is an organization composed of 56 national and international labor unions representing a wide scope of workers in fields ranging from education to mining and from doctors to artists. The federation aids workers in improving their local labor unions and helps to ensure that their voices are heard in discussions about workers rights. The website of Working America, the community affiliate of the AFL-CIO, provides current information about unemployment in the United States, information about services available to those who are unemployed, and updates about the steps being taken to alleviate the problem.

Brookings Institution

1775 Massachusetts Ave. NW, Washington, DC 20036
(202) 797-6000
website: www.brookings.edu

The Brookings Institution, a nonprofit think tank, provides policy recommendations on all issues addressed by the U.S. government. Brookings suggestions are made with the goal of ensuring the continued strength of the American democracy, economic and social well being for the American people, and international cooperation. The institution's position on unemployment calls for the provision of wage insurance for those who have lost their jobs, more progressive allocation of benefits, and incentives to return to work. Articles by Brookings scholars addressing the unemployment situation include "The State of the Job Market, June 2010," "Why Congress Needs to Extend Emergency Unemployment Benefits," and "Job Creation Has Left the Building." These articles and others can be accessed on the Brookings website.

Cato Institute

1000 Massachusetts Ave. NW, Washington, DC 20001-5403
(202) 842-0200 • fax: (202) 842-3490
website: www.cato.org

Founded in 1977, the libertarian Cato Institute promotes the principles of individual liberty and free market economics. Topics addressed by institute scholars include, but are not limited to, the economy, national security, and trade. In their analysis of the current unemployment situation, Cato scholars have denounced the government stimulus allocated to create jobs, charging that it has actually increased unemployment. Articles outlining this stance include "The 'Stimulus' for Unemployment," "A Second Stimulus Package? Yikes," and "Did the Stimulus Work?" Additional views from Cato on unemployment can be found in the institute's publications—the tri-annual *Cato Journal*, the quarterly *Cato's Letters*, and the bi-monthly *Cato Policy Report*.

Center for American Progress (CAP)
1333 H St. NW, 10th Floor, Washington, DC 20005
(202) 682-1611 • fax: (202) 682-1867
e-mail: progress@americanprogress.org
website: www.americanprogress.org

The progressive public policy organization CAP seeks to oppose traditionally conservative ideals by utilizing modern mass communications techniques to reach a broad audience. Specific ideas advocated by the center include the reestablishment of America as a global leader, the proliferation of clean energy technology to benefit the environment and the economy, economic prosperity for all people, and universal health care. CAP's focus on labor and work has centered recently on unemployment in the United States and includes articles and testimony such as "Economic Mismanagement," "Today's Unemployment Crisis by the Numbers," and "Policy Responses to Long-Term Unemployment."

Center for Economic and Policy Research (CEPR)
1611 Connecticut Ave. NW, Suite 400, Washington, DC 20009
(202) 293-5380 • fax: (202) 588-1356
e-mail: cepr@cepr.net
website: www.cepr.net

CEPR utilizes a two-pronged approach to help U.S. citizens better understand and participate in the democratic process. The center first facilitates research on economic and social issues and then presents its findings to the public in a concise, comprehensible manner. CEPR's work on labor and jobs includes the identification and tracking of factors impacting American workers' wages, benefits, and employment opportunities. Reports and commentary featured on the CEPR website addressing unemployment include "The Adult Recession: Age-Adjusted Unemployment at Post-War Highs," "More Stimulus Needed to Reduce Unemployment," and "Public Spending Still Key to Economic Recovery."

Economic Policy Institute (EPI)
1333 H St. NW, Suite 300, East Tower
Washington, DC 20005-4707
(202) 775-8810 • fax: (202) 775-0819
e-mail: epi@epi.org
website: www.epi.org

An organization representing the low- and middle-income workers in the United States, EPI provides a voice for these individuals in both national and international debates concerning economic policy. Every two years, the organization publishes the report *State of Working America*, which analyzes the conditions working Americans face. Issues addressed by the EPI include changes in wages, incomes, and cost of living; health care and education; international trade and economics; and the state of manufacturing and other employment sectors. The organization publishes monthly reports showing unemployment figures as well as articles and commentary offering EPI scholars' analysis of the current employment situation and what can be done to improve it.

Heritage Foundation
214 Massachusetts Ave. NE, Washington, DC 20002-4999
(202) 546-4400 • fax: (202) 546-8328
e-mail: info@heritage.org
website: www.heritage.org

The Heritage Foundation is a conservative public policy organization that promotes policies that espouse the ideals of free enterprise, limited government, individual freedom, traditional American values, and a strong national defense. Heritage scholars have conducted extensive research into the increasing unemployment rate and their research can be found on the organization's website. Offerings include the "Heritage Unemployment Report: June Job Market Jolts Economy," "Unemployment Remains High Because Job Creation Has Yet to Recover," and "A Good Job Is Not So Hard to Find."

Institute for Policy Studies (IPS)
1112 16th St. NW, Suite 600, Washington, DC 20036
(202) 234-9382 • fax: (202) 387-7915
e-mail: info@ips-dc.org
website: www.ips-dc.org

Founded in 1963 as an anti-war and civil rights organization, IPS has shifted its focus through the years to human rights in the 1970s, and recently centered on international peace and justice movements. While international concerns remain a large part of the organization's research, the rising unemployment rate in the United States has become a major issue addressed by IPS. The institute has called for drastic action to be taken by the president to create jobs, as outlined in the article "Jobs Crisis Needs Drastic Action." Additional articles addressing the unemployment situation can be read on the IPS website.

National Employment Law Project (NELP)
75 Maiden Ln., Suite 601, New York, NY 10038
(212) 285-3025 • fax: (212) 285-3044
e-mail: nelp@nelp.org
websites: www.nelp.org, www.unemployedworkers.org

NELP seeks to combat the growing insecurity experienced by the American workforce in the face of globalization and domestic policy changes, two factors that have destabilized employment in the United States. The organization's programs are designed to create good jobs, increase upward mobility, insure the continued observance of workers' rights, and aid unemployed Americans. The website of the organization's project

Laid Off & Left Out, www.unemployedworkers.com, provides specific and timely information about unemployment, action that workers can take to obtain needed benefits, and current legislation dealing with unemployment.

TheMiddleClass.org

40 Exchange Pl., Suite 2001, New York, NY 10005
(646) 274-5700 • fax: (646) 274-5699
e-mail: info@drummajorinstitute.org
website: www.themiddleclass.org

Themiddleclass.org is a website project of the Drum Major Institute for Public Policy (DMI) dedicated to assessing current legislation based on its impact on the middle class. DMI produces annual reports and studies assessing federal policy; themiddleclass.org is a project to provide current information about policy decisions as they are being debated so the American people have the opportunity to affect the legislation that will result in changes in their lives. This website examines current legislation, gives detailed but accessible summaries of the legislation, and then rates the bills based on their impact on the middle class. Issues covered include workplace and job creation, consumers, and debt and bankruptcy.

U.S. Department of Labor (DOL)

Frances Perkins Building, 200 Constitution Ave. NW
Washington, DC 20210
(866) 487-2365
e-mail: cpsinfo@bls.gov
website: www.dol.gov

The U.S. DOL is the government agency dedicated to protecting job seekers, employees, and retirees in the United States by ensuring workers rights, minimum wage, and workers benefits, among others. The DOL provides extensive information for job seekers and those who are unemployed covering topics such as jobs and training, layoff resources, retirement and health benefits, and current employment statistics. Information about unemployment insurance can be found on the DOL website as well.

Bibliography of Books

Bruce Bartlett	*The New American Economy: The Failure of Reaganomics and a New Way Forward*. New York: Palgrave Macmillan, 2009.
Jagdish Bhagwati	*In Defense of Globalization*. New York: Oxford University Press, 2004.
Amy Sue Bix	*Inventing Ourselves Out of Jobs?: America's Debate Over Technological Unemployment, 1929–1981*. Baltimore, MD: Johns Hopkins University Press, 2000.
Benjamin B. Bowser	*The Black Middle Class: Social Mobility—and Vulnerability*. Boulder, CO: Lynne Rienner, 2007.
Edgar K. Browning	*Stealing from Each Other: How the Welfare State Robs Americans of Money and Spirit*. Westport, CT: Praeger, 2008.
William A.V. Clark	*Immigrants and the American Dream: Remaking the Middle Class*. New York: Guilford, 2003.
Thomas J. Cottle	*Hardest Times: The Trauma of Long Term Unemployment*. Westport, CT: Praeger, 2001.
Vox Day	*The Return of the Great Depression*. New York: WND Books, 2009.

Lou Dobbs	*Exporting America: Why Corporate Greed Is Shipping American Jobs Overseas*. New York: Warner, 2004.
Robert H. Frank	*Falling Behind: How Rising Inequality Harms the Middle Class*. Berkeley, CA: University of California Press, 2007.
Charles R. Geisst	*Collateral Damaged: The Marketing of Consumer Debt to America*. Hoboken, NJ: Bloomberg, 2010.
Steven Greenhouse	*The Big Squeeze: Tough Times for the American Worker*. New York: Alfred A. Knopf, 2008.
Bruce C.N. Greenwald and Judd Kahn	*Globalization: The Irrational Fear That Someone in China Will Take Your Job*. Hoboken, NJ: Wiley, 2008.
Thomas F. Huertas	*Crisis: Cause, Containment and Cure*. New York: Palgrave Macmillan, 2010.
William M. Isaac	*Senseless Panic: How Washington Failed America*. Hoboken, NJ: Wiley, 2010.
Vinay B. Kothari	*Executive Greed: Examining Business Failures That Contributed to the Economic Crisis*. New York: Palgrave Macmillan, 2010.
Paul Krugman	*The Return of Depression Economics and the Crisis of 2008*. New York: W.W. Norton, 2009.

Les Leopold, *The Looting of America: How Wall Street's Game of Fantasy Finance Destroyed Our Jobs, Pensions and Prosperity—And What We Can Do About It*. White River Junction, VT: Chelsea Green, 2009.

David Neumark and William L. Wascher, *Minimum Wages*. Cambridge, MA: MIT Press, 2008.

Nomi Prins, *It Takes a Pillage: Behind the Bailouts, Bonuses, and Backroom Deals from Washington to Wall Street*. Hoboken, NJ: Wiley, 2009.

Jack Rasmus, *Epic Recession: Prelude to Global Depression*. London: Pluto, 2010.

Carmen M. Reinhart and Kenneth S. Rogoff, *This Time Is Different: Eight Centuries of Financial Folly*. Princeton, NJ: Princeton University Press, 2009.

Robert J. Shiller, *The Subprime Solution: How Today's Global Financial Crisis Happened, and What to Do About It*. Princeton, NJ: Princeton University Press, 2008.

John F. Wasik, *The Audacity of Help: Obama's Economic Plan and the Remaking of America*. Hoboken, NJ: Bloomberg, 2009.

Index

C

D

E

F

G

H

I

J

K

L

M

N